OCLC record

INTRODUCING

Lacan

Darian Leader + Judy Groves

Edited by

Icon Books

This edition published in the UK in
2005 by Icon Books Ltd.,
The Old Dairy, Brook Road,
Thriplow, Cambridge SG8 7RG
email: info@iconbooks.co.uk
www.iconbooks.co.uk

Sold in the UK, Europe, South Africa
and Asia by Faber and Faber Ltd.,
3 Queen Square, London WC1N 3AU
or their agents

Distributed in the UK, Europe, South
Africa and Asia by TBS Ltd., Frating
Distribution Centre, Colchester Road,
Frating Green, Colchester CO7 7DW

This edition published in Australia in
2005 by Allen and Unwin Pty. Ltd.,
PO Box 8500, 83 Alexander Street,
Crows Nest, NSW 2065

Previously published in the UK in
1995 and Australia in 1996 under the
title Lacan for Beginners and in 2000
under the current title

Reprinted 2001, 2003, 2005

This edition published in the USA in
2005 by Totem Books
Inquiries to: Icon Books Ltd.,
The Old Dairy, Brook Road,
Thriplow, Cambridge
SG8 7RG, UK

Distributed to the trade in the USA by
National Book Network Inc.,
4720 Boston Way, Lanham,
Maryland 20706

Distributed in Canada by
Penguin Books Canada, 90 Eglinton
Avenue East, Suite 700, Toronto,
Ontario M4P 2YE

ISBN 1 84046 669 3

Originating editor: Richard Appignanesi

Printed and bound in Singapore
by Tien Wah Press.

Be wary of the image.

Born on 13 April 1901, Jacques Marie Émile Lacan was the first child of Charles Marie Alfred Lacan and Émilie Philippine Marie Baudry. Alfred Lacan was the Paris sales representative of a large provincial firm. The family lived in comfortable conditions in the Boulevard du Beaumarchais before moving to the Montparnasse area where Jacques entered the prestigious Catholic school, the Collège Stanislas.

An outstanding pupil, he excelled in religious studies and Latin. As a teenager, Jacques Lacan developed a passion for philosophy, adorning the walls of his bedroom with a plan of the structure of Spinoza's **Ethics**, a text which would always remain dear to him and which he would quote at the start of his doctoral dissertation in medicine.

WHILE LACAN WAS BUSY CONSTRUCTING THE PLAN OF SPINOZA'S ETHICS, THIS PAINTING HUNG ON THE WALL IN FREUD'S CONSULTING ROOM IN VIENNA.

The Surrealist Movement

Lacan took up the study of medicine in 1920 and specialized in psychiatry from 1926. During this period, he was active in the busy Parisian world of the writers, artists and intellectuals who made up the Surrealist movement. He frequented Adrienne Monnier's bookshop on the Left Bank, along with the likes of André Gide and Paul Claudel and, at the age of seventeen, met James Joyce.

A friend of André Breton and Salvador Dali, he was to become Picasso's personal physician and a contributor to several Surrealist publications from the early 1930s.

Beginnings in Psychiatry

His internship at St-Anne hospital, starting in 1926, and at the Infirmerie Spéciale des Aliénés de la Préfecture de Police, in 1928, gave Lacan a particular interest in the study of paranoia. Later he would say that . . .

> My only real master in psychiatry was Gaëtan Gatian de Clérambault.

Lacan singled out his concept of **"mental automatism"**. This brought together many seemingly disparate phenomena of madness under the common motif of **something being imposed from "outside"**: the echo of thoughts or a commentary on one's actions, for example.

The form of a particular psychosis would then be determined by how one *made sense* of these elements which lacked an initial content. Lacan would say that this concept was the closest that contemporary French psychiatry got to a structural analysis, with its emphasis on the imposition of formal elements beyond the "conscious" control of the subject.

Paranoia

In 1932, Lacan completed his doctoral thesis on paranoia, **Paranoid Psychosis and its Relations to the Personality**, a study which had a great influence on many of the Surrealists.

I REFERRED TO LACAN'S WORK IN THE FIRST ISSUE OF THE SURREALIST REVIEW, *MINOTAURE*, IN *1933*.
(SALVADOR DALI)

MINOTAURE

I often contributed to MINOTAURE.

I CHAMPIONED THE POETRY OF THE PATIENT, AIMÉE, THAT LACAN DESCRIBED IN HIS *1932* THESIS.
(PAUL ELUARD)

The Case of Aimée

The thesis contains a detailed analysis of a woman, named Aimée after the heroine of one of her unpublished novels, who had attempted to stab a well-known Parisian actress, Huguette Duflos. The case was widely reported in the press at the time, and Lacan tried gradually to piece together the logic behind her apparently irrational act. His thesis introduced a new concept into the psychiatric milieu, that of **"self-punishment paranoia"**. Lacan argued that, in striking the actress, Aimée was in fact striking herself: Duflos represented a woman with freedom and social prestige, exactly the sort of woman that Aimée aspired to become.

In her ideas of persecution, it was this figure that she saw as the source of threats to her and her young son. **The ideal image** was thus both the object of her hate and of her aspiration. Lacan was especially interested here in this complex relation to images and the ideas of identity to be found in paranoia. In her subsequent arrest and confinement, she found the punishment which was a real source of the act itself. She understood, at a certain level, that **she was herself the object of punishment.**

Lacan's analysis of the case shows many of the features which would later become central to his work: **narcissism, the image, the ideal,** and how the personality could extend beyond the limits of the body and be constituted within a complex social network. The actress represented a part of Aimée herself, indicating how the identity of a human being could include elements well outside the biological boundaries of the body. In a sense, **Aimée's identity was literally outside herself**.

Analysis

Around the same time that Lacan completed his thesis, he began his analysis with Rudolph Loewenstein, which continued until 1938. Loewenstein had been analysed by Freud's student Hans Sachs.

FREUD

I LATER EMIGRATED TO THE *USA* WHERE I BECAME WELL KNOWN FOR MY WORK IN ESTABLISHING THE PROGRAMME OF EGO PSYCHOLOGY.

SACHS

LOEWENSTEIN

Studies in Philosophy

Instead of confining himself to the standard texts in psychiatry and psychoanalysis, Lacan read widely, with a special interest in the philosophic work of Karl Jaspers, G. W. F. Hegel and Martin Heidegger. He attended the seminars on Hegel given by Alexandre Kojève together with many of the thinkers who would leave their mark on French intellectual life, Georges Bataille, Raymond Aron, Pierre Klossowski and Raymond Queneau.

Marriage

In 1934, Lacan married Marie-Louise Blondin, the sister of his friend the surgeon Sylvain Blondin. Three children were born from this marriage, Caroline in 1934, Thibaut in 1939 and Sibylle in 1940.

The Marienbad Congress

Lacan made his first intervention at the annual Congress of the International Psychoanalytical Association, held at Marienbad, in 1936. He developed the thesis of the **"mirror phase"**.

But my paper was interrupted by the chairman of the session, Ernest Jones, Freud's biographer.

The original text of this paper is lost, but the brilliant article on the family which Lacan contributed to the *Encyclopédie Française* in 1938, together with a later version of the paper, presents the argument clearly.

Theory of the Mirror Phase . . .

Humans are born prematurely. Left to themselves, they would probably die. They are always born too early. They can't walk or talk at birth: they have a very partial mastery of their motor functions and, at the biological level, they are hardly complete.

I CAN'T PICK THINGS UP OR MOVE TOWARDS OR AWAY FROM THINGS.

So how does the child come to master its relation to its body? How does it respond to its "prematuration"?

. . . and Mimicry

Lacan's answer is in the theory of the mirror phase. He draws our attention, in later texts, to an ethological curiosity, known as **"mimicry"**.

Certain beasts have the habit of assuming the insignia and colouring of their surroundings.

Hence a stick insect may choose to look like a stick. The obvious explanation for this phenomenon is that it protects the animal against predators. But what many investigators found was that those animals which assumed an image or disguise were just as likely to be eaten as those which didn't.

The US government had commissioned a survey in the early 1930s involving the rather macabre task of examining the stomachs of some 60,000 Nearctic birds to confirm this diagnosis by counting the insects which had been swallowed. The ones which had disguised themselves were no less frequent than their more honest companions.

So if evolutionary biology cannot provide an answer to the question of mimetism with the idea of protection from predators, how can it be explained?

Roger Caillois, a French thinker fascinated with the theme of masks, games and the relation of the human to the animal kingdom, argued that there was a sort of natural law whereby **organisms become captured in their environment**. They will thus take on the colouring, for example, of the space around them.

Captured in an Image

Lacan developed this thesis in his work on the mirror phase, combining it with observations from child psychology and social theory and argued for a similar form of imaginary capture for the organism in an external image

The child identifies with an image outside himself, be it an actual mirror image or simply the image of another child.

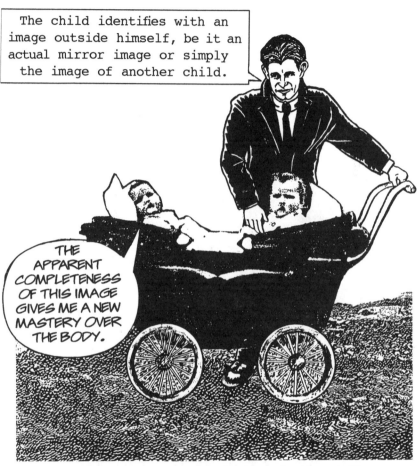

THE APPARENT COMPLETENESS OF THIS IMAGE GIVES ME A NEW MASTERY OVER THE BODY.

In the 1938 encyclopedia article, this idea is used to give a brilliant explanation of the inexplicable swings in a child's behaviour from a tyrannical or seductive attitude to its opposite. Rather than linking this to a conflict between two individuals, the child and the spectator in this instance, Lacan argues that it derives from a conflict internal to each of them, resulting from **an identification with the other party**. This is an organizing principle of development rather than a single moment in childhood. If I have identified with an image outside myself, I can do things I couldn't do before.

The Imaginary

Mastery of one's motor functions and an entry into the human world of space and movement is thus at the price of a fundamental alienation. Lacan calls the register in which this identification takes place "the imaginary", emphasizing the importance of the visual field and the specular relation which underlies **the child's captivation in the image**.

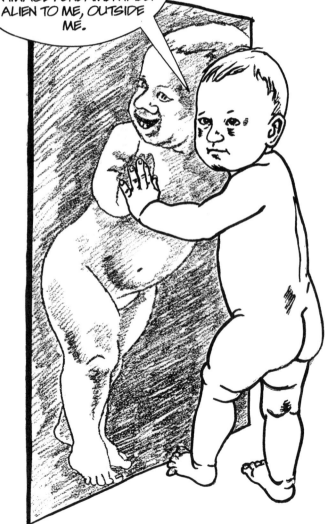

BUT ALL THIS AT A PRICE. IF I AM IN THE PLACE OF ANOTHER CHILD, WHEN HE'S STRUCK, I WILL CRY. IF HE WANTS SOMETHING, I'LL WANT IT TOO, BECAUSE I AM IN HIS PLACE. I AM TRAPPED IN AN IMAGE FUNDAMENTALLY ALIEN TO ME, OUTSIDE ME.

Ego and alienation

Lacan shows how this alienation in the image corresponds with the ego: **the ego is constituted by an alienating identification, based on an initial lack of completeness in the body and nervous system**.

My thesis provided a response to the question posed by Freud in his famous 1914 paper on Narcissism.

If the ego is the seat of narcissism and if narcissism does not exist from the start of life, what must happen for narcissism to emerge?

SOME "NEW PSYCHICAL ACTION" MUST TAKE PLACE TO CONSTITUTE THE EGO, BUT I DIDN'T SAY WHAT THIS WAS.

With the mirror phase, Lacan had found an answer.

Negative Hallucination

If the ego seems whole and complete, beyond it is only the fragmented, uncoordinated state of the body.

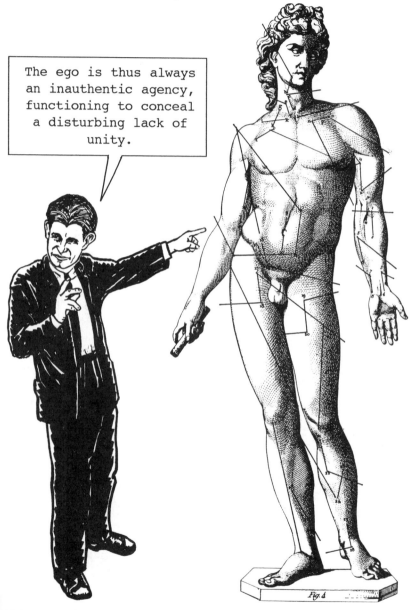

The ego is thus always an inauthentic agency, functioning to conceal a disturbing lack of unity.

Fig. 4

This conception of the ego takes up some of Freud's early ideas.

Freud had been intrigued by the phenomenon known as **negative hallucination**. Subjects would by hypnotized and informed, for example, that there was no furniture in the room. Then they would be requested to fetch something from the far corner of the same room.

The Falsifying Ego

In other words, rationalizations of the hypnotized persons' actions were produced which had the function of glossing over the true state of affairs. Whereas other commentators had drawn attention to this **falsifying character of the ego** in the isolated context of negative hallucination, Freud and Lacan saw it as the basic characteristic of the ego at all times.

As with the ego of the mirror phase, its task is to maintain a false appearance of coherence and completeness.

THUS ANALYSIS MUST BE BOTH MISTRUSTFUL AND SUBVERSIVE OF MATERIAL WHICH STEMS FROM THE EGO DOMAIN.

Any theory of psychoanalysis which involved the idea of the analyst making an alliance or pact with the patient's ego was thus fundamentally ill-starred. It could only result in a mutual deception.

In this early part of Lacan's work, the human subject oscillates between two poles: **the image, which is alienating, and the real body, which is in pieces**. In his work of the 1930s and early 1940s, Lacan often attempts to show the presence of these images of the fragmented body beneath the classic psychoanalytic complexes.

The phantasy of fragmentation may be found beneath the more celebrated phantasy of castration.

He developed the thesis that **in paranoia we can witness a sort of decomposition** which illustrates clearly the stages in the "normal" constitution of the image and of reality as such.

The Construction of the Ego

For example, the motifs of mirrored images, telepathic communication, observation and external persecution so common in paranoia may be understood as fundamental building blocks in the constitution of the ego. If the ego is constructed on an image outside ourselves, if our identity is given in an alienation . . .

The truth of the ego emerges precisely in madness where the world seems to dissolve and the difference between self and other is radically put in question.

In our day-to-day relations with other people, we are unaware of these criteria, even if many works of art, notably those of Dali, try to capture this idea.

I was thus led to the theory that human knowledge is in its very essence paranoiac.

It is in paranoia that we can see so clearly the components, the steps which go to make up the relation to the world which madness can remind us of.

Although Lacan's theory of the image at this date is often explained in terms of the influence of surrealism, it owes much more to certain currents in French psychiatry such as the work of Joseph Capgras and those psychiatric thinkers interested in problems of recognition, doubling and the image. Lacan often returned to the notion of the mirror phase to reformulate it during his teaching. It never stayed static. There is no one theory of the mirror phase in Lacan's work, but several.

29

In the Second World War

With the German Occupation of France, Lacan was called up to serve in the French army and then posted to the Val-de-Grâce military hospital in Paris. A relationship began between Lacan and Sylvia Bataille (née Maklès), whom he was later to marry. She was the wife of the writer and theorist Georges Bataille, although the two had been separated since 1933.

She was well known for her roles in the films of Jean Renoir, the most famous of these perhaps being the heroine in **Une Partie de Campagne**. During the Occupation, Lacan made frequent trips from Paris to the South of France to see her, and in 1941 their daughter Judith was born.

Lacan took the decision not to publish anything during the war years. In 1945, after the war had ended, he visited England for a five-week study trip, described in the article "English Psychiatry and the War" (1947). He had a special admiration, he said, for the English during the war, and he reviewed the work of Wilfred Bion and John Rickman whom he had met during his stay.

They tried to use psychoanalytic ideas in the rehabilitation of army misfits.

Lacan was especially interested in their work with small groups. Rather than being organized around the presence of an authority figure with whom they were supposed to identify, these groups were centred on activities.

A group forms round a task or activity, indicating a different sort of identificatory process.

This sensitivity to problems of identification was praised by Lacan and he claimed that Britain's success in the war was in no small part a consequence of introducing such ideas to the military.

Return to Freud

From 1951, Lacan held a weekly seminar in which he urged what he called a return to Freud.

> I advocated a careful rereading, focusing on the constant reference to language and its functions in Freud's work.

The *Interpretation of Dreams*, the *Project* of 1895, *The Psychopathology of Everyday Life* and *Jokes and their Relation to the Unconscious* all deal with operations which are fundamentally of a linguistic nature, from associations between words to the very structure of symptoms themselves.

Freud had already spoken of **"symptoms joining in the conversation"** as early as 1895.

The pain would indicate that something had been left unsaid, showing how physical sensations themselves could be linguistic, sending a message to be picked up by the analyst.

Symptoms and Speech

> I SHOWED HOW SYMPTOMS AND ACTIONS COULD LITERALLY BE WORDS TRAPPED IN THE BODY.

A woman who wishes to have a child jumps from an embankment, the word she uses for "jump" (*niederkommen*) being identical with the word meaning "be delivered of a child". A man's attraction to women with a "shine" on the nose could be traced to the verbal equivalence between the word for "shine" in German (*Glanz*) and the English word "glance".

A whole neurosis could be organized by words and the relations between them. The case of the Rat Man discussed by Freud shows how a massive network of symptoms, compulsions and actions depended on the links between the words *Spielratte* (gambler), *heiraten* (to marry) and *raten* (instalments). **Words became the very stuff of symptoms, the fabric of the life and torment of human beings.**

Signifiers and Signified

Crucial to Lacan's programme of a return to Freud is the distinction between signifier and signified. According to a well-known definition, **a signifier is an acoustic image** (like a word), **a signified is a concept**. The signified has a kind of priority and we use signifiers to gain access to signifieds: or, put more simply, to say what we mean. A word gives us access to a meaning. The passage from word to meaning seems simple enough. We can ask for some object, the listener will understand our meaning and respond with the object. Language is thus all about communicating with each other. We use words to convey meanings and intentions.

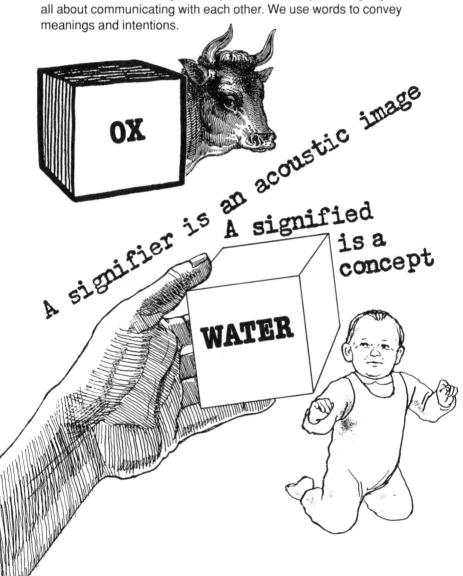

But Lacan saw things differently. Rather than supposing a transparency between signifier and signified, an easy access from word to meaning, he claimed there was a real barrier, a resistance.

A word does not reveal its meaning so simply. Rather, it leads on to other words in a linguistic chain, just like one meaning itself leads to others.

The Rat Man's *raten* does not point to the meaning "instalments" but to other linguistic elements like *heiraten* and *Spielratte*, even though he might not have been aware of these links at all. The group of meanings is organized by the links between the words. There is thus **a priority of the signifier**, of the material, verbal element in psychic life.

Many contemporary board games in which the players have to keep giving the next association of a word or concept show this clearly. Words generate meanings which are beyond the understanding of those who use them. There is a difference between what you mean to say and what your words say. That's why everyday life involves a succession of misunderstandings and apologies.

When Elizabeth I touched her head on her deathbed, what was the message? Did it mean that she was indicating James as her successor or did it mean simply that she had a sore head?

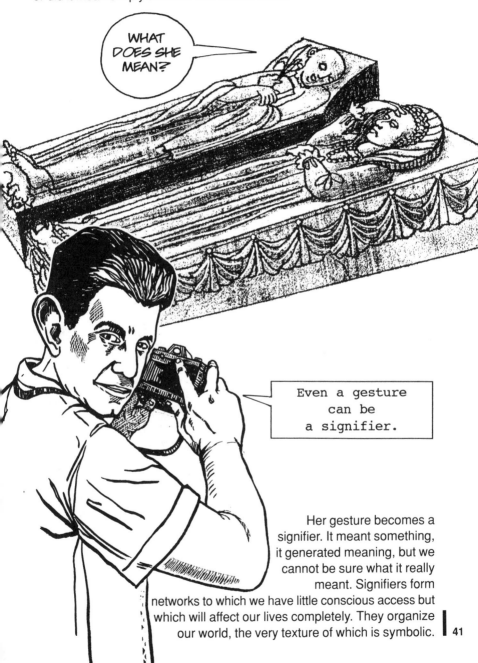

WHAT DOES SHE MEAN?

Even a gesture can be a signifier.

Her gesture becomes a signifier. It meant something, it generated meaning, but we cannot be sure what it really meant. Signifiers form networks to which we have little conscious access but which will affect our lives completely. They organize our world, the very texture of which is symbolic.

The Symbolic

From the start of the 1950s, Lacan stressed more and more in his work the power and organizing principle of the symbolic, understood as the networks, social, cultural, linguistic, into which a child is born. These precede the birth of a child, which is why Lacan can say that **language is there from before the actual moment of birth**. It is there in the social structures which are at play in the family and, of course, in the ideals, goals and histories of the parents. Even before a child is born, the parents have talked about him or her, chosen a name, mapped out his or her future. This world of language can hardly be grasped by the newborn and yet **it will act on the whole of the child's existence**.

This idea has obvious consequences for the theory of the mirror phase. If Lacan had first stressed the *imaginary* identification, he now discussed its *symbolic* side. If the child is captured in an image, he or she will still assume signifiers from the speech of the parents as elements of identification. As a mother raises the baby to see its reflection, she might say . . .

YOU'VE GOT GRANDMA'S EYES.

YOU LOOK JUST LIKE YOUR FATHER.

These are symbolic pronouncements since they situate the child in a lineage, in a symbolic universe. **The baby is bound to its image by words and names**, by linguistic representations. A mother who keeps telling her son "What a bad boy you are!" may end up with either a villain or a saint. **The identity of the child will depend on how he or she assumes the words of the parents.**

The Ideal

There is thus an identification which is both beyond and in a sense prior to the identification with the image: a **symbolic identification with a signifying element.**

If narcissism is about one's relation to one's image, this shows how narcissism is not only imaginary but includes a symbolic dimension as well.

Lacan calls this **an identification with the *Ideal*,** a term which is not intended to suggest anything perfect or literally "ideal". This ideal is not conscious. The child does not suddenly decide to put himself or herself in the shoes of some ancestor or family member. Rather, the speech which he or she hears as a child will be incorporated, forming a kernel of insignia which are unconscious. Their existence may be deduced from clinical material. Analysis reveals the central identifications, how **the subject has "become" what a parent prophesied** or how he or she has repeated the mistakes of a grandparent.

Bertrand Russell was thunderstruck one day to come across one of his father's diaries in a desk drawer which revealed details of his parents' courtship.

This shows the symbolic operating beyond the conscious control or understanding of the players involved, and Russell's surprise shows that the unconscious was really at work.

The key to the theory of identification here is that symbolic identification with an *ideal element* removes the subject from being completely at the mercy of the imaginary images which captivate him or her. They come from another register, the symbolic, and thus serve to ground the subject, to give him a base, in this structure.

The narcissistic imaginary register which Lacan had elaborated in such detail in his early work is now shown to rest on a symbolic foundation: **the relation to the image will be structured by language.**

MY RELATION WITH MYSELF IS CONSTRUCTED "FROM THE OUTSIDE". I LEARN WHO I AM BECAUSE OTHERS TELL ME.

Images are caught up in a complex symbolic web which manoeuvres them, combines them and organizes their relations.

Ego Ideal and Ideal Ego

Hence, Lacan's differentiation of *ego ideal* from *ideal ego*, two terms which we can find at some points in the work of Freud. In Lacan's formulation of 1953, **the ideal ego is the image you assume and the ego ideal is the symbolic point which gives you a place and supplies the point from which you are looked at**. If you drive a car fast, it might be because you assume the image of some racing driver. You identify with him, and this would involve the ideal ego. But the real question is, **who is it that you are identifying with this racing driver *for*?**

This is the dimension of the ego ideal. Clinically, pointing out to a patient an ideal ego identification usually has little effect: to dislodge it, an appeal

must be made to the symbolic dimension, to the register of the ego ideal.

Structuralist Linguistics

What characterizes the symbolic register here is something very particular. Thinkers influenced by developments in linguistics had the idea that any structure is a linguistic one if it has the simple quality of being based on a system of differences. **A word is a word because it is different from other words:** "cat" has its value because it is different from "mat", "fat" and "cot", for example. Or, to move outside the realm of spoken language, a railway network can perfectly well count as a linguistic system since the 10.30 train will still be the 10.30 train even if it arrives at 10.40, precisely because it is different from the 10.00 train and the 11.00 train. **It takes on its value because it is an element in a system of differences.**

The key here is to remember that even if the carriages are changed every day, the 10.30 train is still the 10.30 train. What matters is not the "content" of the train but its place in an overall system.

Thus **the central property of a linguistic system is
*discontinuity***, the existence of a series of differential elements.
Discontinuity means gaps: there is a space between elements. The
10.30, 11.00 and 10.00 trains do not all arrive at the same time and they
are not all superimposed on the railway timetable.

This discontinuity is set in opposition by Lacan to the imaginary register
which strives to avoid the dimension of lack or absence. This endeavour
is of course inauthentic, since the imaginary itself is based on a serious
and troubling form of discontinuity, **the gap between the child's
uncoordinated body and the envelope of the whole image
which it assumes**.

The Unconscious and Language

If the ego is imaginary, the unconscious for Lacan is structured like a language: that is, it is constituted by a series of chains of signifying elements. Like an infernal translating machine, it turns words into symptoms, it inscribes signifiers into the flesh or turns them into tormenting thoughts or compulsions. **A symptom may be literally a word trapped in the body.** Remember that all that children really know about their internal organs is what their parents tell them. The inside of their body is thus made up of words. Doctors are familiar with patients who complain of pains when a biological cause is clearly absent. This does not mean that the pain is false: it is exactly the same pain, perhaps even a greater one, as if it were caused by some real physical determinant.

To relieve the pain, the repressed ideas need to be linked to the rest of the signifying chain. They have to undergo a new translation.

This shows how **a symptom is made up of words**. And just as the study of language reveals the presence of many different linguistic mechanisms, the study of symptoms gives the same results.

A METAPHOR INVOLVES THE SUBSTITUTION OF ONE ELEMENT FOR AN-OTHER, FOR EXAMPLE, "LION" FOR "BRAVE MAN".

This is the very structure of the symptom — one term is substituted for another, which is kept repressed.

When it is connected with the rest of the chain of words, there will be an effect on the symptom. Linking the signifier "to wake up on the wrong side of the bed" with the apparent symptom is a translation which both removes it – in this case – and produces new material.

The Variable Session

Lacan's sensitivity to discontinuity led to a radical change which he introduced into the practice of psychoanalysis. Whereas his contemporaries worked with an average 50-minute session, Lacan made the length variable.

I NEVER KNOW WHEN THE SESSION IS GOING TO END . . .

The session is stopped on an important word or phrase, and the patient is then left to meditate on this until the next session. This technique has several advantages over the standard 50-minute session.

Psychologists had been aware for some time of a peculiar effect known as the Zeigarnik effect, which demonstrated that interrupted activities **produced more associative material than completed ones**. A tune broken off in the middle would evoke more than one played until the end. Anyone with a tape recorder is aware of this.

This capacity of interruption to generate memories and associative material forms one part of the rationale of the variable session. The broken sessions may evoke the broken Oedipal love relations.

There is also the effort to avoid suggestion or, in everyday language, brainwashing the patient. Thus, instead of being offered a running commentary on the analytic material, the patient himself or herself is, through the breaks in the sessions, allowed to do much of the work.

Variable time is invaluable in combating many forms of resistance, such as the common one of patients' preparing their sessions in advance.

In the atmosphere of a variable session, there is a certain degree of tension – one does not know when it is going to end – and this tension serves to generate material and upset standard patterns of resistance. To understand what a variable session is about, one has to experience it, as the real experience of time which it introduces is startling, disturbing and completely unexpected.

Lacan tells a story in 1953 about his use of variable sessions.

It allowed me to escape a patient's interminable discourses on the art of Dostoyevsky — which produced the phantasy of anal pregnancy resolved by caesarean section.

And he said much more. H... ...t more and more drunk, and became very maudlin, ...st lachrymose. Masloboyev had always been a capital f... ...w, but cunning, and as it were precocious; he had bee... ...shrewd, crafty, artful dodge... from his school-days by... ...n the whole he was not altogeth... bad; but he was a los... ...an. Among the Russians there a... many such men. ...ey often have great abilities, h... everything seems ...gled up in them, and what's more th... are quite capab... of knowingly acting against their co... science in certa... cases through weakness, and not only co... to inevitable ...uin, but know beforehand that they are on t... ...ruin. Masloboyev, for one, was drowning himself...

The dimension of discontinuity and rupture introduced by the variability of the length of the sessions was thus effective in **generating the most hidden material**.

Speech and Language

Lacan elaborated on his conception of the relations of the imaginary and the symbolic in his famous Rome Discourse of 1953, "The Function and Field of Speech and Language in Psychoanalysis".

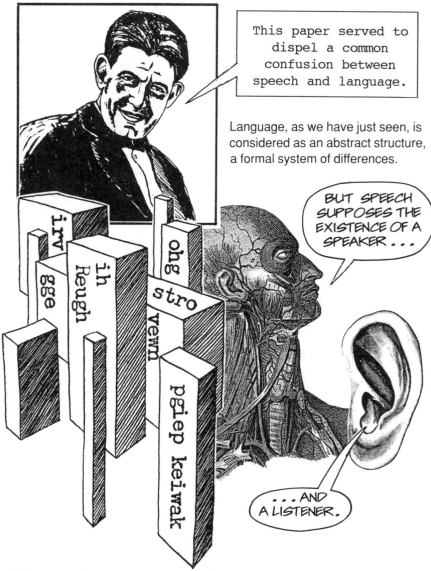

This paper served to dispel a common confusion between speech and language.

Language, as we have just seen, is considered as an abstract structure, a formal system of differences.

BUT SPEECH SUPPOSES THE EXISTENCE OF A SPEAKER . . .

. . . AND A LISTENER.

If language is a structure, **speech is an act**, generating meaning as it is spoken and giving an identity to the speakers involved.

Saying "You are my master" gives a signification to the position of the speaker: either as the slave, or, more likely, as someone who does everything apart from accept the position of slave. Speaking thus determines one's position as speaker, **it gives one a place**. As a patient speaks, such significations will emerge which are unconscious.

THE WORDS I USE MEAN MORE THAN I MEAN IN USING THEM.

They carry meanings which are beyond his or her conscious understanding and control. As the analysis continues, the message can be sent back to the patient.

The subject receives the message in inverted form. His desire can finally become recognized.

At this point in his work, Lacan thought that speech had a subject who strives for the recognition of his or her desire. Since speech usually has the opposite effect, that of blocking recognition, this is hardly an obvious outcome.

And if recognition is seen as central to a theory of how speech works, it supposes the existence of an Other, **a place from which you are heard, from which you are recognized**.

The Other is thus the place of language, external to the speaker, and yet, since he or she is a speaker, internal at the same time.

To the extent that Lacan associates speech and the symbolic, it is possible for the subject to be recognized, to find some kind of identity, in the symbolic order.

The Real

To the symbolic and the imaginary, Lacan adds the category of the Real, something he reformulated at several moments in his work. In 1953, **the real is simply that which isn't symbolized**, which is excluded from the symbolic. As Lacan says, the real "is that which resists symbolization absolutely". He calls **the real, the symbolic and the imaginary the "three registers of human reality"**. Thus, what we ordinarily speak of as "reality" would best be defined as an amalgam of symbolic and imaginary: imaginary to the extent that we are situated in the specular register and the ego offers us rationalizations of our actions; and symbolic to the extent that most things around us have meaning.

Everyday objects are symbolized in the sense that they mean something, they have a signification.

SOMETIMES AN OBJECT LOSES ITS MEANING. I LOOK AT AN EVERYDAY OBJECT AS IF IT IS MYSTERIOUS AND UNCANNY.

The real would represent precisely what is excluded from our reality, the margin of what is without meaning and which we fail to situate or explore.

The Psychoanalytic Institution

In 1953, Lacan, together with many colleagues, left the *Société Parisienne de Psychanalyse* (SPP) to form the new group, the *Société Française de Psychanalyse* (SFP). Lacan did not agree with the standardized form of practice which the SPP was doing its best to introduce.

> Nor did I see eye to eye with the SPP on the question of psychoanalytic training.

Leaving the SPP to form the SFP had the consequence, unknown to Lacan and his colleagues, of depriving them of membership of the International Psychoanalytical Association, and, in the following years, a complex process of negotiation was to take place to determine the status of the new group.

In his work of the early 1950s, Lacan saw the image as the central source of resistance in psychoanalytic treatment. **The ego is made up of privileged images and the task of analysis is to dissolve them.** They must be integrated in speech and the symbolic network, rather than remaining stagnant and inert, blocking the dialectical progression of speech.

The initial step in analysis is to reveal not what the patient is saying, but from where they are speaking — to reveal where their imaginary alienation is situated.

Understanding what someone is saying must come after this.

When the patient says "I", the analyst should be mistrustful! "I" must be separated from the "ego". The "I" of speech might seem to refer to the person sitting in front of you, but this is not the same thing as the ego, the site of the imaginary identifications.

When a patient says "I", the analyst shouldn't be fooled!

It is necessary to see from where he is speaking, perhaps the place of a sibling, a friend or a parent who has been identified with at an unconscious level.

Ego and Subject

Lacan introduced the distinction between the ego and what he called the subject. **The ego is imaginary, whereas the subject is linked by Lacan to the symbolic.** It is a fundamentally split or divided entity: split by the laws of language to which it is subordinate, and split to the extent that it does not know what it wants.

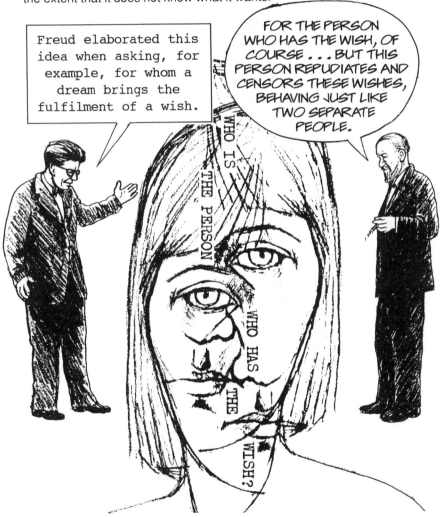

Freud elaborated this idea when asking, for example, for whom a dream brings the fulfilment of a wish.

FOR THE PERSON WHO HAS THE WISH, OF COURSE ... BUT THIS PERSON REPUDIATES AND CENSORS THESE WISHES, BEHAVING JUST LIKE TWO SEPARATE PEOPLE.

WHO IS THE PERSON WHO HAS THE WISH?

Freud's *The Interpretation of Dreams* is a book not just about dreams but about dreamers. This divided subject does not have any one representation, but emerges rather at moments of discontinuity: for example, in a slip of the tongue or a bungled action.

Examples of Neurosis: 1. The Hysteric

Neurosis itself, Lacan thinks, is a sort of question asked by the subject by means of the ego. The identification is used to ask a question. For the hysteric, this question is: **what is it to be a woman?**

Dora complains of her father's affair and yet seems extremely anxious that it continue.

Her real centre of interest is femininity. She'll identify, although not consciously, with a man, in order to pursue this inquiry.

WHAT INTERESTS ME IS INVESTIGATING MAN'S DESIRE. WHAT DOES A WOMAN HAVE IF SHE CAN MAKE A MAN LOVE HER, BEYOND THE DIMENSION OF SEX?

SHE IDENTIFIES AT THE LEVEL OF THE EGO WITH *MR K*, THE MAN NOT ONLY MARRIED TO *MRS K* BUT WHO DESIRES DORA HERSELF.

She repeats the relation with Mr K that her father has with Mrs K: to be desired but without having complete sexual relations. She can thus study the desire of the man, what it is that a man desires in a woman.

Examples of Neurosis: 2. The Obsessional

For the obsessional, the question is: **am I alive or dead?** He will spend his life never acting, but waiting. When he has a problem, he won't get on the telephone, but will brood and think interminably. His life is mortified by rituals, habits, rules. When it comes to action, he would rather that someone else act in his place, thus avoiding any real vital struggle with another living being. An example of this is the way in which many men will push the woman they love towards their best friend.

LIVING OUTSIDE MYSELF IN THIS WAY, I BECOME A SORT OF LIVING CORPSE.

Freud had linked this picture to an unconscious resolution of a problem with the father.

RATHER THAN REALLY FIGHTING THINGS OUT, THE SON IMAGINES HIS FATHER IS ALREADY DEAD?

My version focuses on the place of the ego here. The obsessional not only awaits the death of his master, but identifies with the master as already dead. Hence the mortified quality so common in obsession.

I LIVE MY LIFE ACCORDING TO STRICT ROUTINES AND DAILY RITUALS, AVOIDING ANY EN—COUNTER WITH SEXUALITY NOT ORGANIZED BY MYSELF.

Like the soldier who plays dead on the battlefield so as to avoid any real confrontation with death, the obsessional's position is a paradoxical one. Cheating death implies a living mortification.

Structural Anthropology

It is the task of analysis, Lacan argues, to indicate to the subject the place of the ego and to turn the stagnatory images which captivate him into part of the associative material. **Analysis thus involves the full assumption by the subject of his or her history:** the images of the ego have to be integrated into this symbolic text. Analysis is thus a passage to the symbolic at this moment in Lacan's work, and he is continually elaborating his theory of this register with input from other fields, structural anthropology in particular.

My friend, the anthropologist Claude Lévi-Strauss, was engaged in similar research at the time.

I SHOWED HOW SYMBOLIC STRUCTURES WHICH ARE NOT CONSCIOUSLY PERCEIVED CAN ORGANIZE AND GOVERN THE WORKINGS OF A SOCIETY, AND, INDEED, THE MIND OF THE INDIVIDUAL.

$$(M+y+A)\, M \sim m$$

$$\left(\frac{I}{M+y+\alpha}\right) M \sim m + \pi$$

$$p(M)(M') \sim \left(\frac{\alpha}{y}\right) \pi$$

Lacan was especially interested in Lévi-Strauss's use of the mathematical group, a theme which he returned to several times in his own work.

$$M_3(p=m) = f\left[M_2 \begin{smallmatrix}(p=p)\\(m=n)\end{smallmatrix}\right]$$

$$f\left[M_2 \begin{smallmatrix}(p=p)\\(m=m)\end{smallmatrix}\right] = f\left[M_1(p=m)\right]$$

$$f(a,b,c,d) \equiv (a+1, b+1, a+c+d+1, d+p)$$
$$g(a,b,c,d) \equiv (a+1, b, a+c+q+1, d+q)$$

A → B
C → D
Generalized exchange

$$A\left\{\begin{smallmatrix}1=1\\2\ \ 2\end{smallmatrix}\right\}B$$

$$C\left\{\begin{smallmatrix}1=1\\2\ \ 2\end{smallmatrix}\right\}D$$

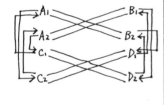

Mathematical Models

During the 1940s and 1950s many new mathematical methods had been introduced into anthropology: algebraic structures, structures of order and topologies. What interested Lacan in the early and mid 1950s was the algebraic side. An equation in mathematics could be associated with a group of permutations, and group theory is the part of mathematics which pays special attention to the properties of such groups.

> I had the idea that a neurosis might obey laws which could be studied in exactly the same way — that it might consist of a group of rules for permutation.

An initial situation – such as the details of the marriage of one's parents – would be transformed into certain rules in one's own life, completely unconsciously, to generate situations – such as one's own marriage or love life – which both repeated the initial situation and transformed it in important ways. The laws of this transformation process could be given the same mathematical formalization that anthropologists like Lévi-Strauss were employing.

Lacan's contact with structural anthropology was also to result in a revision of the classical psychoanalytic theory of the Oedipus complex.

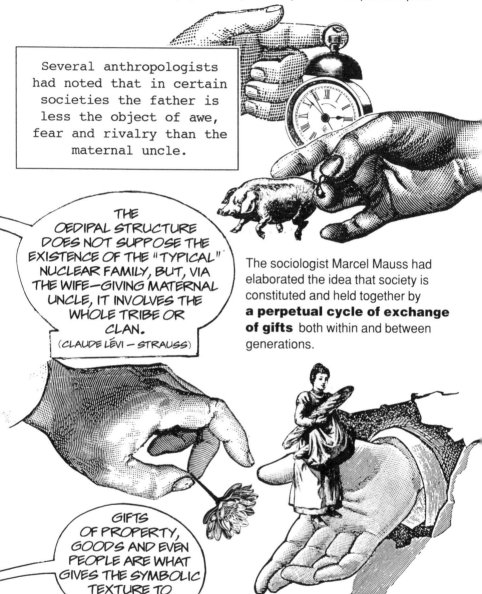

Several anthropologists had noted that in certain societies the father is less the object of awe, fear and rivalry than the maternal uncle.

THE OEDIPAL STRUCTURE DOES NOT SUPPOSE THE EXISTENCE OF THE "TYPICAL" NUCLEAR FAMILY, BUT, VIA THE WIFE—GIVING MATERNAL UNCLE, IT INVOLVES THE WHOLE TRIBE OR CLAN. (CLAUDE LÉVI — STRAUSS)

The sociologist Marcel Mauss had elaborated the idea that society is constituted and held together by **a perpetual cycle of exchange of gifts** both within and between generations.

GIFTS OF PROPERTY, GOODS AND EVEN PEOPLE ARE WHAT GIVES THE SYMBOLIC TEXTURE TO SOCIETY. (MARCEL MAUSS)

72 The giving itself rather than what you give is the key factor. It is symbolic.

The Name of the Father

Now, from these theories, it follows that a marriage will serve to cement relations in the community and will make of the man and woman involved mere players in a larger symbolic organization. A marriage involves a whole community and not just the immediate relatives and parents. **The man and woman thus become part of a symbolic chain.** The real, biological father is thus to be distinguished from the symbolic structures which organize the relation of man to woman. Paternity has a symbolic side to it, and Lacan called this agency of paternity **the name of the father. It is not a real person but a symbolic function**.

This should not be confused, as it often is, with the real name of the father. It is merely a term to designate the symbolic side of paternity as opposed to its real nature, reduced in the modern world to sperm. A woman can become pregnant today without having had sexual intercourse with a man: artificial insemination is made possible by science, a fact which still illustrates the Lacanian distinction between real and symbolic agencies.

Artificial insemination involves the sperm — and, crucially, also the symbolic side, in the form of scientific discourse, an organized symbolic structure with its own laws and powers.

The Phallus

Now, Lacan argues that the Oedipus complex will result in the child's entering the symbolic circuit and moving away from the immediate relation with the mother. This relation, however, is not a dual one. It does not involve simply mother and child.

> There are three terms present: the mother, the child and the object of the mother's desire — what I call "the phallus".

Once this triangular structure is established, the child can try, with the many games of seduction that children are so good at, to become this third term, the object of the mother's desire. **It is an attempt to be the phallus for the mother**, to incarnate the phallus in whatever form is particular to the individuals in question.

The Symbolic Network

Lacan argues that this imaginary object of the child's games must be transported to the symbolic level. **The images which the child uses to entice the mother must be given up**, marked with the sign of prohibition. Now, this is where the anthropological stress on the role of giving in society becomes so important.

He or she will be able to leave the universe of the mother to take on a place in the larger universe of the symbolic world. The imaginary object must take on the value of a gift, and hence the crucial time of the Oedipus complex will involve establishing this new signification. **The phallus will be the object promised to the child for use in the future**, it will become the object of a pact.

SOME DAY, THIS WILL ALL BE YOURS . . .

This promise supposes, of course, that what will be returned in the future has been taken away first. Assuming a sexual position thus supposes an initial loss or subtraction.

Lacan's theory of the Oedipus complex will be reformulated later on in his work, as we shall see.

Is Lacan a Structuralist?

By the late 1950s, Lacan's work shifts its focus from the problem of speech to the problem of language. Speech is an act, involving subject and other. **Language**, however, **is a structure**: as such, it does not suppose a subject. There is nothing human about a language, if it is seen as **a formal system of differences** and distinguished clearly from speech.

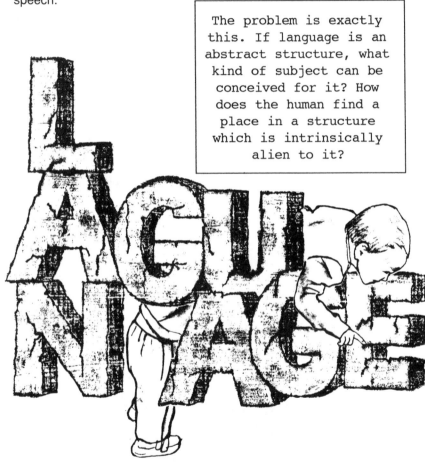

The problem is exactly this. If language is an abstract structure, what kind of subject can be conceived for it? How does the human find a place in a structure which is intrinsically alien to it?

Lacan is thus hardly a **structuralist**. Structuralism aimed to do away with the subject and the notion of subjective agency, putting in its place the autonomy of linguistic structures. As Jacques-Alain Miller has pointed out, although Lacan shares this conception of the autonomy of the symbolic, he is deeply concerned at the same time, to find a place for the subject here.

Try writing a small ad: "Nice young man who likes going to the theatre . . ." What you write is different from you. It may represent you, but in being so represented, you have to confront the fact that words are not there to help you. **They have not been designed for you**, and yet you have to find your way around in the world of language in order to survive.

There is thus a new theory of alienation in Lacan. The early work referred to alienation in the register of the image, and now **alienation is situated in the register of language**. If speech was first seen as giving the subject some sort of identity, now **language has the role of blocking identity**. This is the difference between Lacan's conception of language in 1953 and that of 1958: the subject is no longer recognized but abolished.

Loss and Language

From early childhood, you have to use speech to express your needs. But the minute you use words to express something, you are in another register. If you need water, asking for it changes things.

THE WATER MATTERS LESS THAN WHETHER MY MOTHER GIVES IT TO ME.

IN OTHER WORDS, HOW I MANIFEST MY LOVE.

The object of need becomes pulverized by the dimension of language: what matters now is not the object, the water, but the sign of love. **Speaking thus introduces a particular form of loss into the world.** To speak is to make the object vanish, since one is speaking to someone else.

The object of need becomes eclipsed in the demand.

Desire

Demand is ultimately a demand for love, and, for this reason, unsatisfiable. If someone asks you if you love them and you say yes, that will not stop them from asking you again and again and again. The impossibility of really proving one's love once and for all is well known. Hence demand is a continuing spiral. But Lacan adds something more. To need and demand, he adds the register of desire. **Desire takes up what has been eclipsed at the level of need** (the dimension represented by the mythical water) and introduces an absolute condition in opposition to the absolutely unconditional nature of demand.

We can see this in cases where human desire literally has an absolute condition, in fetishism.

I CAN ONLY REACH SEXUAL ENJOYMENT WHEN A PARTICULAR OBJECT OR TRAIT IS PRESENT IN MY PARTNER, LIKE A RIBBON OR A CERTAIN PAIR OF BOOTS.

Enjoyment is determined strictly by the presence of this element.

And Lack . . .

Although the example of fetishism is an extreme one, Lacan shows that it is at the horizon of all desire for the man. A man's choice of partner will always contain some reference to inhuman details: the colour of the partner's hair, her eyes etc. There is nothing "human" about such abstract features. **Desire is thus linked to conditions** in contrast to the register of demand.

> Part of the work of analysis is to try to tease out the subject's desire from his incessant demands. The neurotic is someone who privileges demand, who hides his desire beneath the imposing presence of demand.

If demand is demand for an object, desire has **nothing** as its object: nothing in the sense of "**lack taken as an object**". Some clinical structures show the difference clearly. The anorexic, for example, in refusing to eat gives a place to desire beyond demand. To the mother's demand for the child to eat, the latter offers a symbolic refusal, maintaining a desire centering on the "nothing" which is eaten. Into the relation with the mother, a lack is thereby introduced, **something which marks out clearly the tension between demand and desire**.

Desire and Wish

Desire itself will emerge in little details, and hence Lacan's insistence on hunting it down, on **searching for desire in between the lines**, where it is least obvious. The emphasis on detail here is fully Freudian. After all, Freud had shown that when an unconscious current is repressed, since it cannot enter consciousness, it displaces itself on to tiny details and it is only in following these derivatives that we will mobilize the rest of the complex in question.

It is important to distinguish what Lacan calls desire from what we would ordinarily call a wish. **A wish is something you want consciously.** But desire is fundamentally barred from consciousness. Freud had made the distinction earlier in his work on dreams. A dream may represent some obvious wish. You are freezing and starving in the middle of the North Pole. You fall asleep and dream of a fine four-poster bed and a bowl of caviar.

It would seem that the dream fulfils a wish, to find food and shelter. But **this wish is only an alibi**: what really matters is why, in your dream, the supposed fulfilment has taken the form of a four-poster bed and a bowl of caviar.

WHY NOT JUST A NORMAL BED? WHY NOT A BOWL OF HOT SOUP?

Desire is different from the wish here.

Desire is simply equivalent to the process of distortion which has turned the wish for shelter and food into this particular image, these particular details. If you dream of passing an exam in a certain place the night before sitting a real exam, desire is more likely to be found not in the idea of passing the exam (a wish) than in the **detail** of the place in question (why this place rather than another?).

Distortion and Desire

Desire is thus a very peculiar thing. Lacan elaborates a theory of desire as something very strange, very odd: it has nothing to do with wishes, but consists of linguistic mechanisms which twist and distort certain elements into others. A slip of the tongue would provide another example. You say one thing instead of something else and you do not know why. **Desire is present because one element has been distorted and modified by another one.** We can deduce the presence of desire in clinical work by paying attention to these processes as they repeat themselves and to the points of rupture, distortion and opacity in a patient's associations.

WISH TO FIND FOOD

A bowl of caviar

AND SHELTER

A four-poster bed

If language has a capacity to transmit a message, it also has a redundant side. It's the difference between a letter and a telegram. The telegram conveys the minimum information content quickly, whereas the letter may dwell on details, use rhetorical devices and bow to the requirements of etiquette. Now, if we aim to track down desire, Lacan says, we will do best by **focusing not on the message, but rather on the points of redundancy**, the little details which do not really need to be there. Why a "bowl of caviar" rather than just "caviar"?

The Maternal Phallus

If desire here is a process of distortion, a force at work in between signifiers, how can we speak about an object of desire? It would seem, on the contrary, as if desire did not have any object. Lacan replies that the object is of a very particular kind: **an absent one.** It is not any absent object but, for Lacan at this moment in his work, a very precise one: **the maternal phallus.**

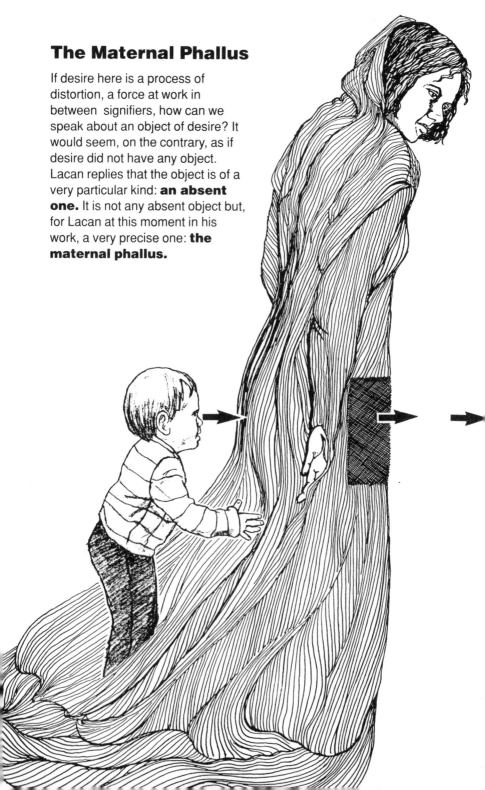

Freud and his followers, despite many disagreements, had always stressed the centrality of the castration complex. The key is less the possession by the subject of a phallus, but whether the mother has one or not.

THE PHALLUS IS NOT THE SAME THING AS THE PENIS: IT IS THE PENIS PLUS THE IDEA OF LACK.

If you think that you might lose your penis and that other people do not have this organ, the idea of loss will become linked to the organ in question. It will never be a penis again. In Freudian theory it will be **a penis plus the idea of its absence**. Hence what one searches for in the mother cannot be seen: how can one see something which is not there?

The Missing Phallus

The neurotic wants, in Lacan's terms, to be the phallus for the mother. The child is searching for some object, but it is a lost one, as the intervention of the father in the Oedipus complex prevents the child from assimilating itself with the object of the mother's demand. The intervention of the father distances the child from the mother, it gives the child possibilities of leaving the universe of the mother. And **it situates the phallus as something lost, forever out of reach**. It says "No" both to the child and to the mother.

NO!

As something missing, the phallic object is best represented by a veil or something which covers or conceals. How else can a lack be represented, after all, than by the image of a screen which points to something beyond itself? Later on in his work, Lacan would modify this conception. We will discuss it shortly, but it is important first to fill in some of the detail of this picture of the Oedipus and castration complexes.

The Oedipus Complex . . .

The child is at the mercy of the mother at the start of life, dependent on her in all senses of the word, and unable to understand the rationale of her behaviour. However marvellous or cruel the mother may be, the same question will pose itself for the child, a question which concerns him or her to the quick: **what does she want?**

These are all questions which can preoccupy a child, and the answer the child gives to them will form a crucial part of the Oedipus complex. We should note that for some children, on the contrary, these questions fail to be posed for a simple reason: there is no space for the child to ask them. The mother is literally with her child constantly, failing to evoke the dimension of absence or lack. The child cannot question the mother's desire because, in a sense, he or she is the object which saturates her, the object to which her whole existence is reduced.

If, however, the mother does show that her life is not completely reduced to the child, things are otherwise. **The child is confronted with a series of questions about the mother's movements and whims.** Lacan argues that there is an operation which will link all these enigmas about the mother to a precise signification, that of the phallus.

Melanie Klein (1882–1960) had seen how, out of all the objects that the child situates in the mother, one is special, privileged – the father's penis. Lacan gave a new formulation to this idea with his theory of the phallus.

There is always something beyond the child to which the mother's desire is directed. This, Lacan argues, is the phallus, something forever out of the child's reach and beyond its own capacities to incarnate.

The Castration Complex

Now, how does castration fit into all this? We cannot stress enough that one of Lacan's most important achievements was to make the theory of the castration complex central once again in psychoanalysis. This had, of course, been a constant reference for the first and particularly the second generation of Freud's followers, but by the 1950s it was quite unremarkable to find a whole theoretical article or a case report which made absolutely no mention of this crucial Freudian concept.

> I elaborated the idea that the child tries to be the phallus for the mother.

If the Oedipal process works properly, the child will give this up, the phallus becoming less an imaginary object than **a signification of what is missing**.

Confronted with this loss, boys and girls have certain options.

His use of the sexual organ must be based on the acceptance of the fact that there is a symbolic phallus always beyond him, which he does not have but may one day receive in the future.

I CAN ACCEPT HAVING THE PHALLUS — BUT ONLY IF I ACCEPT THAT *HAVING* IS BASED ON A PRIOR *NOT-HAVING.*

I CAN ACCEPT NOT HAVING THE PHALLUS — BUT ONLY IF THE ORIGINAL PHALLIC IDENTIFICATION WITH MY MOTHER IS RENOUNCED.

She may entertain a nostalgia for the lost phallus or hope to receive it in the future from a man. Whereas Lacan puts **having** on the side of the man, he puts **being** on the side of the woman. Being the phallus in this context means literally being a signifier, which explains, for example, the propensity to masquerade which Joan Rivière had seen as the key feature of feminity.

It is important to distinguish at least two different conceptions of the phallus in Lacan's work of the 1950s. Firstly, as an **imaginary** object, an imaginary lack which can circulate and upon which the sexual games of children are so often based. And, secondly, **as a signifier**, a symbol of desire, which is different from the question of having or not having a penis. It is literally a symbol, representing the enjoyment that has been lost in getting through the Oedipus complex. Failure to distinguish imaginary and symbolic may lead to the greatest clinical confusion in work with patients.

A Clinical Example

Here is an example from Lacan's practice. A man finds himself impotent. He hatches a scheme which he proposes to his mistress.

That night, she has a dream which she recounts to him in the morning.

On hearing this dream, Lacan's patient immediately recovers his potency and performs magnificently there and then. Now, how does the dream show the distinction between the phallus as an imaginary object and as a signifier?

The man is clearly trapped in a kind of imaginary muddle. He situates the potency, the phallus, on the side of another man, the one who will sleep with the mistress.

And yet this does not stop her from desiring one, showing the man that the phallus is a signifier, separate here from any question of having or not having a penis. It signifies desire and the dimension of what we do not have, what is lacking, something which cannot be identified with having or not having the imaginary object.

The Phallus and Language

Even more startling is the link Lacan establishes between this symbol and language itself. In using speech, the child sees its object vanish: the glass of water becomes secondary to whether the mother responds or fails to respond to the demand. **Speaking thus separates us from what we want.** Entering the register of language, of the signifier, does this not by chance but by necessity: it is a structural feature of language that **it will distort whatever message we have**. This is no doubt the reason why children play Chinese Whispers. One child whispers a message to another and it travels around the circle of children, only to be revealed by the last member of the chain.

WHEN IT'S HEARD, THE DIFFERENCE BETWEEN THE END PRODUCT AND THE ORIGINAL MESSAGE IS AMAZING!

The phallus represents what we lose in entering the world of language — the fact the message will always be slipping away, that what we want will always be out of reach because of the fact that we speak.

The game shows how language works, how the initial element is altered, the circle of children incarnating the network of language. Lacan argues that **the symbol of this process of distortion is the phallus**.

The Name of the Father

How is this symbolic operation of the phallus linked to the father? It is by her speech that the mother situates a reference to a father who is beyond her, which need not be identical with the real father, as long as it serves to separate mother and child. Lacan calls this structural, symbolic element **the name of the father**. The father is a name because ultimately paternity always involves something beyond the biological reality of the man who gives his sperm, something purely symbolic to which Christian culture gives a famous representation. The Virgin Mary gives birth without any real sexual relation with the Divinity, showing how paternity must not be reduced to the register of biology. We see this also in the common belief in many cultures that a woman's pregnancy is linked to her having passed by a certain sacred place. **There is always this disassociation between the real side of paternity and its symbolic side.**

THE NAME OF THE FATHER

$$\frac{\text{NAME OF FATHER}}{\text{DESIRE OF MOTHER}} \rightarrow (-\varphi)$$

The Oedipal operation is called by Lacan the "**paternal metaphor**". It is a metaphor since it involves the substitution of one term for another, **the name of the father for the desire of the mother**. The result of the operation is a **signification**, that of the phallus as lost or negated. We remember that for Lacan the structure of metaphor involves substitution, and a substitution always generates a signification – in this case, the phallic one. The key to all this lies in Lacan's revision of the classical theory of the Oedipal father which we have discussed in part.

The father for Lacan is not the real father, the man who comes home at 5 p.m. and watches television. Rather, **he is a symbolic function**, less a person than a place, which is responsible for separation from the mother. When the child picks up on the key place of the phallus for the mother, he or she will try to incarnate this object for her, although knowing full well that he or she is not identical with it. Hence, a child might try to be everything for its mother.

I WANT TO ENCHANT OR PUZZLE HER, SEDUCE ALL THE ADULTS AROUND ME, BECOME REALLY SOMETHING FOR HER.

The child is trying to be the object which it thinks the mother lacks. The phallus is just the name for this object: that which the mother lacks. Once this definition is accepted, it can be noted in **a very wide range of clinical forms**.

IT MIGHT MEAN BEING A GLOWING, SEDUCTIVE CHILD . . .

. . . OR IT MIGHT MEAN BEING A DEAD ONE — WHATEVER FORM SEEMS TO INTEREST THE MOTHER MOST.

"Being the phallus" refers to an imaginary position and not to any one specific behaviour pattern. Each analysis shows the particular form it takes for different people

The paternal operation is to destroy this game with the mother, to signify that the phallus the child wishes to incarnate is lost, that it is out of the child's reach, that it is missing.

I HAVE TO CONFRONT THE FACT THAT NOT SIMPLY AM I POWERLESS TO INCARNATE IT, BUT THAT THIS IS IMPOSSIBLE.

When I refer to the phallic signification in the paternal metaphor, I am referring to the signification that the phallus, for both sexes, is lost.

This is castration, the renunciation of the sustained attempt to be the phallus for the mother. Neurotics are people who have unfortunately not committed themselves to this renunciation.

The real father may have the task of incarnating this symbolic dimension of this name of the father, but he is by no means identical with it. This is seen clearly in the one-parent family.

I CAN HAVE A SUPERB OEDIPUS COMPLEX, EVEN IF THERE'S NO REAL MAN AROUND?

WHAT MATTERS IS HOW I SITUATE SOMETHING BEYOND MYSELF, HOW I SIGNIFY AND TRANSMIT TO MY CHILD THE FACT THAT THE WORLD DOESN'T BEGIN OR END WITH IT.

In other words, what matters is how she manages to indicate, implicitly, to the child the existence of a symbolic network to which they are both linked, a network which is beyond the imaginary relation of the two of them.

The Structure of Psychosis

Lacan's study of the symbolic function led him to a brilliant formulation of the structure of psychosis in his essay "On a Question Preliminary to Any Possible Treatment of Psychosis".

> The name of the father is simply absent from the mental universe of the psychotic patient.

It literally does not exist there. Freud had remarked on several occasions that there must be a mechanism peculiar to paranoia which differed radically from such well-known mechanisms as repression or denial found in hysteria, obsession or perversion.

Lacan took a term from Freud's text to name this mechanism:
foreclosure (*Verwerfung*), designating a radical rejection of the
element in question.

When an element is
repressed, it can
return in one's speech,
in the signifying chain,
the symbolic.

But when an element is
foreclosed, it can't
return in the symbolic,
for the very simple
reason that it never
existed there in the
first place. It was
rejected, banished.

THE NAME OF

Hence, it returns not in the symbolic but **in the real**:
for example, in the form of hallucinations.

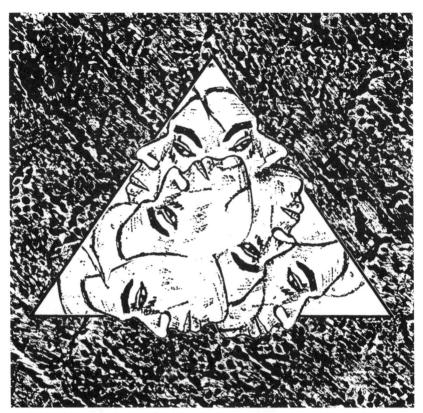

The Triggering of Psychosis

In psychosis, Lacan showed, there is a foreclosure of the name of the father: it is not repressed, but completely obliterated. This hypothesis explained clinical data in a dazzling new way. Analysts and psychiatrists had often noted the presence of the motif of paternity and filiation in psychotic delusions, as seen in the ubiquity of Trinitarian and religious motifs, but now Lacan provided not only an explanation but a refined theory of what was going on in delusion. He showed how careful inquiry into the triggering of a psychosis indicated as its catalyst **an encounter with some situation which evoked for the subject the idea of paternity**. For example, becoming a father for a man, or having one's baby handed to one after birth for a woman. Or, a promotion in one's work or a change in one's symbolic status in the world. All these situations make a call to the register of symbolic paternity, but since there is nothing there, **the subject is confronted with a hole, a gap**. Hence the common sensation of the "end of the world" noted in the early stages of a psychosis.

The subject faces the lack of a signifier, that of the name of the father, and, consequently, the lack of a signification. We remember that for Lacan, the signifier produces the signified. Therefore, the absence of a signifier means absence of a signified. What a psychotic delusion does, according to Lacan, is try to supply precisely this missing signification in the place of the hole opened up by the absence of the name of the father. A delusion, after all, gives a meaning to the world.

IT'S CLOUDY TODAY BECAUSE OF AN ALIEN PLOT TO CONTROL THE WEATHER.

THE RANDOM NOISE I JUST HEARD IN THE STREET IS A SECRET TRANSMITTER BEING ACTIVATED.

In other words, a delusion can serve as a way of giving sense to the menacing world around one, made menacing precisely by the absence of certain fundamental significations to give an order to it.

The delusional signification replaces the standard, Oedipal one. Hence, the common themes in delusion of filiation and of heritage: as the dimension of paternity fails to be encoded in the symbolic, **it returns in the real**. The presence of filiation motifs in the psychotic delusion thus shows how the idea of paternity returns in the real. Contrary to the practice of many of his contemporaries, Lacan did not refuse to see psychotic patients.

The study of paranoia remained one of my life-long research interests.

The Logic of Psychosis

Thus, just as Freud had argued that a delusion is an attempt at self-cure, Lacan saw it as a secondary effect, **an attempt to provide a meaning to the primary problematic of foreclosure**. This idea is also implicit in the theory of mental automatism. The psychotic subject has to make sense of everything that is imposed on him and, as Clérambault had claimed, **he does this using reason**.

IF HE REALLY HEARS VOICES WHEN THERE'S NO ONE THERE, IT'S ONLY REASONABLE TO LINK THEM TO THE TELEVISION SET, FOR EXAMPLE. IN ANOTHER CENTURY, THEY MAY HAVE BEEN LINKED INSTEAD TO SPIRITS.

Thus delusions use the knowledge of the time to provide meanings, a fact which is seen in the change in delusional motifs from one epoch to another.

Lacan goes further here than his master in psychiatry. Madness is not simply a product of reason, **it is an exercise of the most rigorous logic**. The construction of the delusion may follow a chain of logical deduction which is much purer than in a neurosis. A man is in love and he eats his lover.

THIS IS PERFECTLY LOGICAL. IF YOU LOVE SOMEONE, YOU WANT TO INCORPORATE AND BECOME ONE WITH THE LOVED ONE.

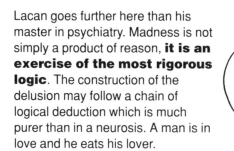

In a neurosis, this sort of logic may be present but in a confused and muddled form.

FOR EXAMPLE, IT MAY TAKE ON THE FORM OF A SYMPTOM: FEELING VERY HEAVY OR PLAGUED BY STOMACH ACHE.

It emerges with clarity in madness. What seems incomprehensible and irrational in psychotic behaviour may turn out to make perfect sense, once the implicit logic is brought out.

The Graph of Desire

In the 1960 text "Subversion of the Subject and Dialectic of Desire in the Freudian Unconscious", Lacan elaborates his famous **Graph of Desire**, a formalization of the dynamics of the unconscious and the drives. On the lower level, we find the imaginary pairing familiar from the mirror phase theory: **m is for "moi", the ego; i(a) for the image of the other**. The relations with the specular image are inextricably bound up with speech and how the mother or care-giver situates the child. Yet, however much the mother speaks, children do not understand language from the day they are born! It takes time to give a signification to the various elements of the speech of the adults surrounding the child. At the start, it is literally a foreign language.

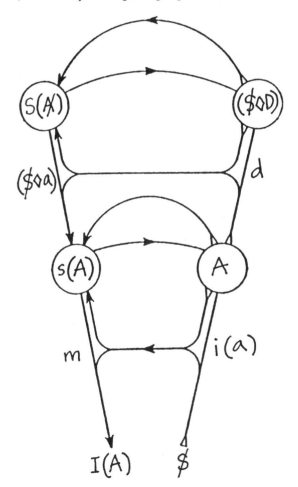

One can, perhaps, experience this profound otherness of language when one travels to a foreign country where not a word of one's mother tongue is spoken. It is indicative of the helplessness of the baby in relation to what will become, later, its own mother tongue.

LANGUAGE IS FIRST OF ALL A FOREIGN ONE.

The Symbol (A)

Now, the set of linguistic elements and their **otherness** is given the symbol **(A)** by Lacan. Significations are gradually set in place for the child, as he or she gradually manages to associate meanings with the signifiers emitted by the adults: whether these are "right" or "wrong" is irrelevant.

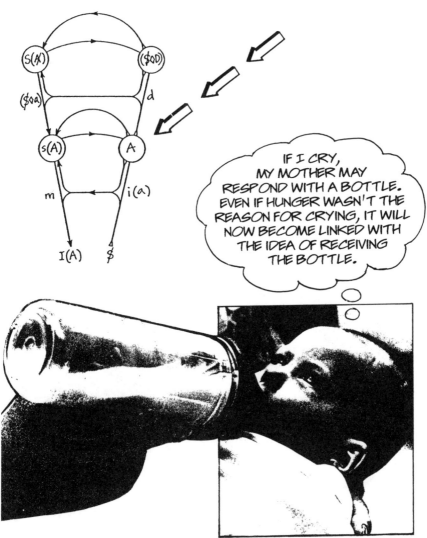

IF I CRY, MY MOTHER MAY RESPOND WITH A BOTTLE. EVEN IF HUNGER WASN'T THE REASON FOR CRYING, IT WILL NOW BECOME LINKED WITH THE IDEA OF RECEIVING THE BOTTLE.

Signification is thus imposed on the child rather than transmitted by him or her.

Symbols (A) and *s*(A)

Likewise, meanings are attributed to the mysteries and enigmas of the mother's speech, gestures, activities. All these count as signifiers for the very simple reason that they are not understood.

ANYTHING IS A SIGNIFIER IF IT SIGNIFIES SOMETHING — BUT I DON'T KNOW WHAT!

The significations established are written by Lacan as **s(A)**. Hence there is an arrow on the graph going from (A) to *s*(A).

Symbol *d* and $ ◇ D

But, as Lacan insists, the speech and behaviour of the adult can never be completely reduced to a signification. There will always be *something*, however marginal, which we do not understand.

How ever much meaning is attributed to the Other, the margin of its desire – **of what we do not understand** – will be present. This is written by Lacan as ***d***, desire of the Other. There are thus two arrows going from (A), one linked to what we understand *s*(A) and one linked to what we do not understand *d* in A. $ ◇ D designates the drive. As certain parts of the body take on a special value in the child's relations with the parents, the drives are established. They are not biologically like instincts but generated by the demands D (eat! shit!) of the parents.

S(Ⱥ): Signifier of the Impossible

S(Ⱥ) indicates the fact that ultimately there is no solution to the question of what we do not understand at the level of language. There are no words to respond to the central questions of sex and existence. Whatever the parents tell the child about these things, the child knows that what they say is inadequate. **S(Ⱥ) designates this point of impossibility**. But Lacan does not simply write (Ⱥ), which would refer to a gap in the Other, in the set of linguistic elements. Instead there is S plus a "barred" (Ⱥ), indicating, paradoxically, **that there is a signifier of the very impossibility of signifying something** – a marker pointing to an impossibility. This is a crucial clinical point. It emerges in analysis at those moments, for example, when there is a very real presence of some sort of logical problem or paradox, something linked to the possibilities of signifying as such.

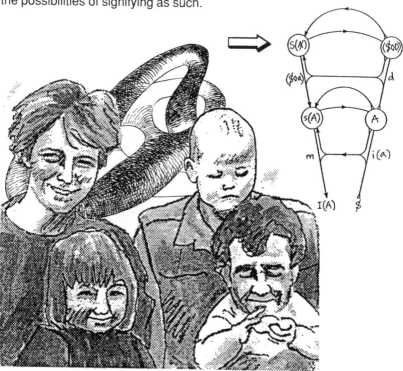

The emergence of S(Ⱥ) is a point in analysis of the utmost horror. A man comes to analysis with a dream in which he is trying unsuccessfully to turn a peculiar elastic shape into a symmetrical object. The shape seems to contain a horrifying dark abyss. He associates with this some half-baked ideas about ordering the relations in his family.

A Clinical Example

Much later in the analysis, the same motifs re-emerge in a new dream, this time involving the search for an object he cannot find.

The dream images translate into the signifier "a circular square", which **indicates a point of logical impossibility**. Without going into the details of the rest of the case material here, we can note how the powerlessness linked to the earlier dream has now been linked to a precise signifier, a signifier indexing the impossibility of finding what he was looking for and condensing in itself a formal impossibility (a circular square). This expression is a true signifier to the extent that it is hardly simple to visualise. It is cut off from the lure of images and easy referents.

S(Ⱥ): Link to Phantasy

S(Ⱥ) is, moreover, a point linked to the phantasy, the next formula to be found in the graph. The desire of the Other is not an abstract issue for the child, but a burning question.

> IF I AM CONFRONTED WITH THE ENIGMATIC DESIRE OF THE **OTHER**, I WILL FEEL AN UNBEARABLE ANXIETY, SINCE I DON'T KNOW WHAT IT WANTS.

If the paternal metaphor answers the question, "What does the mother want?" with the signification of the phallus, there is still the question

"***What am I* for the Other?**" This is a question about existence.

The response to this question is what Lacan calls **the phantasy**. Phantasy is the child's response to the question, "What am I, what place do I occupy for the Other?" It involves assuming the identity of some object given a privileged value in relation to the mother, the sort of object which Anglo-Saxon psychoanalytic terminology would call "pregenital": the breast, excrement and, Lacan adds, the look or the voice.

These objects are particularly interesting since all of them have a kind of dual status, or, more precisely, they have both real and symbolic coordinates. They index the passage from real to symbolic. How?

The Real Object

Note that all of these objects are used in games or rituals with the mother. **The breast** can be turned towards and then turned away from (refusal to eat). **Excrement** can be retained or expelled. **The look** can be hidden or shown (peekaboo). **The voice** can be absent or made terribly present as in the prolonged screaming of many children. Thus all these elements become involved in games of presence and absence, a sign that they are linked into the symbolic and the system of differences.

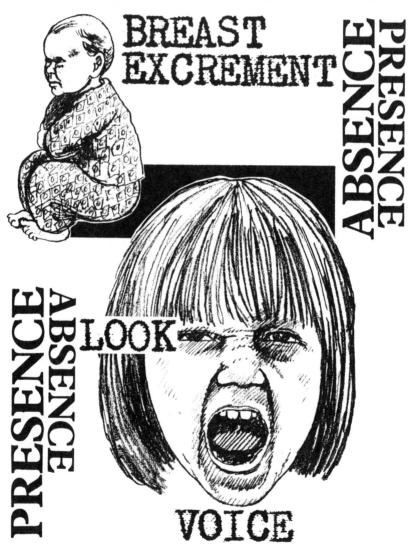

BREAST
EXCREMENT
PRESENCE
ABSENCE
PRESENCE
ABSENCE
LOOK
VOICE

Parent's speech relations with their children tend to centre on these objects and the associated edges of the body. Indeed, they provide the privileged points by which the body is situated in the symbolic, in the register of presence and absence. All mothers know that at a certain moment, children become less interested in any one object as such than in playing with the object, dropping it and then picking it up – in other words, **linking the very fabric of the object itself to the register of presence and absence**.

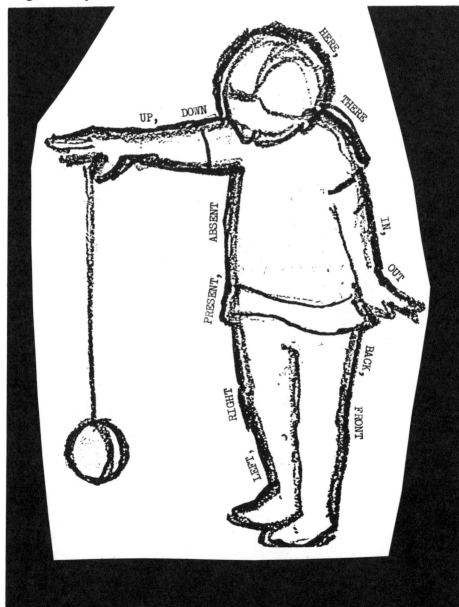

Lost Objects

But these objects at the same time have their non-symbolic side to them. The very fact that they become taken up in the symbolic implies that they are, in themselves, lost or out of reach. They are all rejected, in a sense, by the symbolic. All of them include the dimension of **loss**.

The breast is first of all a part of the child, not of the mother, cut off from the mother as a part of the feeding baby and lost for the child, not just in the weaning, but to the extent that its separation evokes the primary loss of the amniotic envelopes at birth . . .

often to the great anxiety of the small child.

MY LOOK IS THE ONE THING I CANNOT SEE IN MY REFLECTION.

It is cut off from our relation to the rest of the visual field.

THE LOOK

THE VOICE

MY VOICE IS WHAT I DON'T HEAR.

If you try listening to yourself speaking, you become confused. The voice is the signifying chain minus effects of meaning. Part of the body outside oneself, it can return in a terrifying way in the auditory hallucinations of psychosis. These objects all condense unconscious enjoyment in different ways: the mother who watches her child obsessively with an evil eye shows how the enjoyment may be condensed in the look, and the parent who organizes the child's world around the potty shows the condensation in the anal object. The object, although lost, thus includes within itself the **presence** of an enjoyment.

The Phantasy Remainder

Lacan's idea is that in phantasy the child finds a kind of fixity or stability by invoking one of these objects as real, not as a circulating object in the symbolic register, but as a remainder, **a left-over scrap of the whole operation of entering the symbolic.** The subject's mode of exclusion in relation to the signifying chain is seen as equivalent to the exclusion of bits of the body in question. The child establishes a correspondence or homology between two forms of exclusion. Thus, a bit of the body is put into the place where words are missing.

AN INTERNATIONAL PANEL OF DISTINGUISHED ARTISTS WAS ASKED TO PROVIDE AN ILLUSTRATION OF OBJECT (a). HOWEVER THEY ALL AGREED WITH LACAN THAT IT DOES NOT HAVE A SPECULAR IMAGE. SORRY.

Entering the world of language and the symbolic implies parting with the autoerotic relation with parts of my body. It involves a price to be paid.

And now, in phantasy, the child clings to that left-over scrap, that element which promises him or her some sort of identity in a world in which the signifier fails to do this.

Identity

Language does not provide us with a proper identity: the words we use are used by other people, on television, in books, in the media. **The words do not belong to us.** They are alienating. Even when we want to say something intimate, linked to our heart, like "I love you", we might be inhibited because we have heard so many other people say this.

IT IS AS IF THE WORDS ARE THE PROPERTY OF SOMEONE OR SOMETHING ELSE.

THEY BELONG TO THE *OTHER*.

I LOVE YOU, DARLING!

Formula for Phantasy

Confronted with this failure of words to designate our being, what we are, the subject invokes the one object which he thinks escapes the alienating circuits of speech, *the object a*, the remainder from the operation of becoming a speaking being. Hence, Lacan writes the phantasy as (**S**◇***a***), indicating the link of the subject and the object.

Now, once this basic phantasy is established, the child has a sort of compass or rule for his or her life. Lacan calls it an "absolute signification".

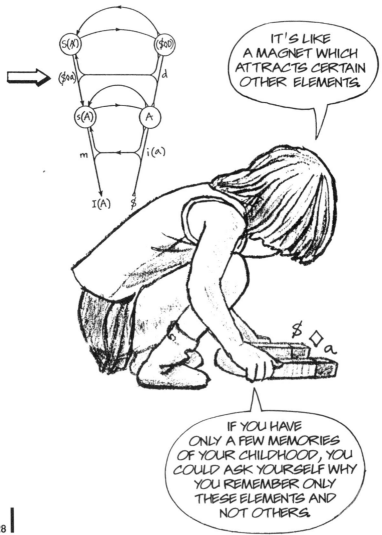

IT'S LIKE A MAGNET WHICH ATTRACTS CERTAIN OTHER ELEMENTS.

IF YOU HAVE ONLY A FEW MEMORIES OF YOUR CHILDHOOD, YOU COULD ASK YOURSELF WHY YOU REMEMBER ONLY THESE ELEMENTS AND NOT OTHERS.

The phantasy is a sort of magnet which will attract those memories to itself which suit it. Likewise, it will play a large part in determining your unconscious identifications.

Even if you have never met the person in question, the magnet of the phantasy is greedy to pick up things overheard or read about. The unconscious identifications which really matter will thus be nourished by the phantasy. Hence the arrow in the graph which goes from ($\mathcal{S}\Diamond a$) to identifications I (A).

Clinical Implications

This theory of phantasy has important clinical consequences. If in analysis we want to have some effect on the subject's relation to his or her phantasy, and, if the phantasy is originally a response to something obscure, opaque, mysterious in the mother, surely the sensible clinical strategy is to try to introduce the same sort of enigmatic thread into the treatment itself.

The analyst refrains from giving explanations and providing meaning to what the patient is telling him. **Offering knowledge would only have the effect of blotting out the dimension of desire.** And if desire is what we find in the gaps in speech, running in between the lines, it would be disastrous to attempt to get rid of the dimension completely.

IF I LEAVE ANALYSIS AFTER THE ANALYST HAS GIVEN SOME GREAT INTERPRETATION, IT IS ASSUMED I LEFT OUT OF RESISTANCE.

This is no doubt often true, but the patient might have left for the very legitimate reason that he or she understood that this wasn't the place where desire could be elaborated.

Hence, Lacan's advice to separate subject from knowledge, rather than trying to solder them together and produce a patient who knows everything as quickly as possible. **The "x" of desire must be kept operative rather than extinguished.**

Creon and Antigone

In his seminar of 1959–60, "The Ethics of Psychoanalysis", Lacan elaborated on this key place of desire in clinical practice.

I contrasted the positions of Creon and Antigone in the ancient Greek drama by Sophocles, ANTIGONE.

Antigone persists in her desire to bury her brother Polynices, whereas Creon offers many reasonable arguments to stop her and to leave the body of this outlaw unburied.

But Antigone remains faithful to her desire. She even goes as far as to bury the body not once but twice, an insistence which she knows will bring death upon her. She thus gives up the comfort of Creon's palace and all the other material benefits of her existence in order to follow through a desire. Creon only wants the good. He wants things to keep ticking along smoothly.

Lacan's comparison serves to distinguish two different positions of the analyst: the one aiming at the good, at regulating problems; and the other, much more frightening, at remaining true to desire.

It is only in psycho-analysis that the ancient ethical problem — "have I acted in conformity with my desire?" — can properly be raised.

This unwillingness to compromise and sensitivity to the dimension of desire which Lacan always advocated was to have an important consequence in the psychoanalytic movement not long afterwards.

The Founding of
the École Freudienne de Paris

In 1963, Lacan was struck off the list of training analysts of the Société Française de Psychanalyse (SFP). His practice and theoretical elaboration were seen as too threatening and challenging for those who opposed him in the established hierarchy, the International Psychoanalytic Association. As a result, he left St-Anne Hospital, the usual venue for his seminars, to move to the École Normale Supérieur, the élite higher education establishment in Paris which has produced generation after generation of France's intellectuals. This move cut short what would have been Lacan's year-long seminar theme of "The Names of the Father". All that remains is the one session he did give on the topic. Soon, Lacan would found a new school, the EFP, first called École Française de Psychanalyse and then the École Freudienne de Paris, which attracted to its ranks the brightest of the École Normale's students, together with many of the old members of the SFP. At the École Normale, he turned to tackle the problem of what he saw at that time as "The Four Fundamental Concepts of Psychoanalysis" . . .

The unconscious, repetition, the drive and transference.

Transference and Supposed Knowledge

The theory of transference broke new ground. Lacan developed a notion of transference as being addressed first of all to knowledge. When we have a dream or make a slip of the tongue, we probably do not understand its meaning and yet we know very well that this meaning, whatever it may be, concerns us.

Transference involves, in part, the attribution of a subject to this knowledge, so that the patient realizes that there is a knowledge he or she is separated from and then assumes that this knowledge has a knowing subject, identified with the analyst.

The analyst is thus the subject "supposed to" a knowledge. **Once this operation of supposition is established, there is transference.** How different this conception is from the standard, classical idea of transference, whereby you behave to someone who resembles your mother or father as you would to them.

I make transference less a consequence of whether your analyst looks like your Ma or Pa, than of SPEAKING itself.

THE MORE I FREE-ASSOCIATE, THE MORE I AM CONFRONTED WITH THE KNOWLEDGE I AM SEPARATED FROM . . .

Transference and the Object

But, as Lacan shows, there is another side to transference which involves something opposed to knowledge, *the object a*. The more the subject is alienated in language, the more his words are uttered faster than he intends, the more slips he makes: in other words, the more he is losing himself in free association . . .

THE MORE I CLOSE MYSELF ROUND THE PHANTASY OBJECT — "THE OBJECT a" — THE OBJECT I THINK WILL GIVE ME SOME ANCHORING FOR MY BEING OUTSIDE THE FIELD OF SPEECH . . .

. . .the more transference works in the direction of the opening up of the unconscious, the more material it produces, the more the object will emerge to BLOCK and OBSTRUCT this production!

Separation

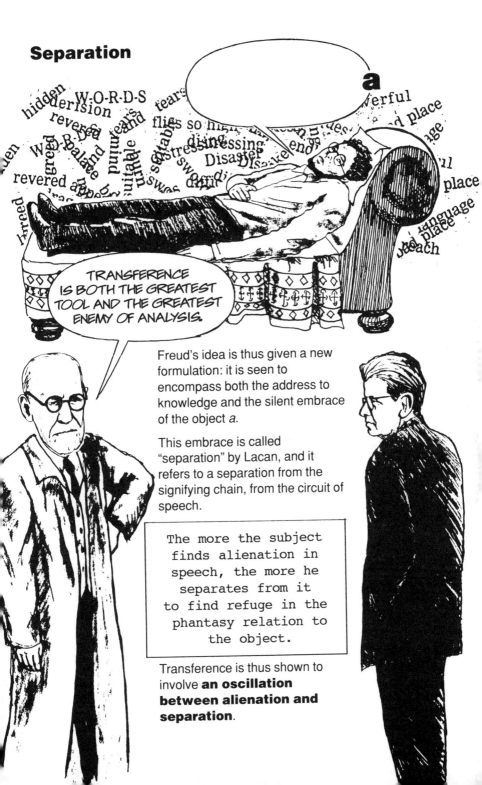

TRANSFERENCE IS BOTH THE GREATEST TOOL AND THE GREATEST ENEMY OF ANALYSIS.

Freud's idea is thus given a new formulation: it is seen to encompass both the address to knowledge and the silent embrace of the object *a*.

This embrace is called "separation" by Lacan, and it refers to a separation from the signifying chain, from the circuit of speech.

> The more the subject finds alienation in speech, the more he separates from it to find refuge in the phantasy relation to the object.

Transference is thus shown to involve **an oscillation between alienation and separation**.

Jouissance

Lacan's work in the 1960s became increasingly concerned with trying to formulate a logic of what he called **jouissance**, a word which is in fact part of English literary heritage, appearing in Edmund Spenser's *Faerie Queene* and other writing of the 16th century. It may mean "enjoyment", as it is usually translated, but in general it is Lacan's way of referring to **anything which is too much for the organism to bear**.

TOO MUCH EXCITATION, STIMULATION OR, PERHAPS, MUCH TOO LITTLE, AS MIGHT BE SEEN IN CERTAIN INERTIAL STATES.

Jouissance is felt 99 per cent of the time as unbearable suffering.

THE PROBLEM IS THAT WHAT WE EXPERIENCE AS UNBEARABLE SUFFERING IS EXPERIENCED BY THE UNCONSCIOUS DRIVES AS, ON THE CONTRARY, A SATISFACTION.

It is *real*, in the Lacanian sense of the word, something outside symbolization and meaning, constant and always returning to the same place to bring you suffering.

Repetition

Freud and his early followers had come to the conclusion by the early 1920s that psychic life was not just reducible to the linguistic formulas and mechanisms of the unconscious. One could interpret a symptom brilliantly, but it would not go away! It refused to budge.

I WAS LED TO THE IDEA OF THE EXISTENCE OF A SILENT FORCE IN THE ORGANISM WHICH WAS INTENT ON SELF-DESTRUCTION, FEEDING OFF THE SUFFERING WE FEEL CONSCIOUSLY.

He linked this to the compulsion humans have to repeat things.

After all, it is a fact that people continue making the same mistakes, the same ill-starred decisions throughout their lives which bring them pain

and grief.

There is no learning from the past for most people, precisely because it is in their very best interests to suffer. Jouissance is thus the real opponent in psychoanalytic practice, and Lacan approached it conceptually in a number of different ways. **The field of psychoanalysis was thus by no means occupied only by language.** The real has now become central in the form of jouissance, real to the extent that it is outside meaning and signification. A different, deadly and heterogeneous presence was at work – jouissance – showing how Lacan's work cannot be reduced, as it often is, to emphasising the importance of language. It is the *relation* of language to jouissance that has now become the central research problem.

To go back to Lacan's early work, Jacques-Alain Miller has pointed out how we can find the characteristics of jouissance in the place given to the imaginary register in the early 1950s: an inertia, something that blocks the progress of free association, something lethal. But now Lacan dissociates his idea of jouissance from the register of the image.

It is working silently and invisibly to bring about its destructive aims.

Although it operates more silently in neurosis, it emerges from its shadowy domain to invade the life of the psychotic, overwhelming the schizophrenic in his or her body, or the paranoiac in his or her ideas of persecution. In paranoia, jouissance is linked to something outside.

Regulating Jouissance

Human life now comes to have a definite purpose: to regulate jouissance. We are born with jouissance in the body, a surplus excitation or bombardment of stimulation which the organism has to rid itself of. As we grow older, **it is drained from the body**: weaning, education, the rules and regulations of the social world . . .

THE *OTHER* INSISTS THAT I MUST SITUATE MY BODY IN A SYSTEM WHICH TELLS ME WHAT AND WHEN TO DO CERTAIN THINGS.

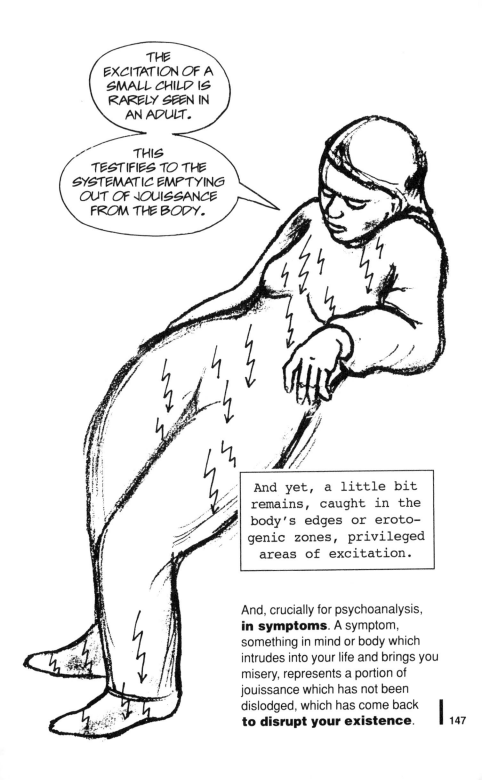

THE EXCITATION OF A SMALL CHILD IS RARELY SEEN IN AN ADULT.

THIS TESTIFIES TO THE SYSTEMATIC EMPTYING OUT OF JOUISSANCE FROM THE BODY.

And yet, a little bit remains, caught in the body's edges or erotogenic zones, privileged areas of excitation.

And, crucially for psychoanalysis, **in symptoms**. A symptom, something in mind or body which intrudes into your life and brings you misery, represents a portion of jouissance which has not been dislodged, which has come back **to disrupt your existence**.

147

Language and Castration

Jacques-Alain Miller has shown how these considerations led Lacan to a new formulation of castration: **the emptying out of jouissance from the body**. And what is the agent of this castration? The symbolic register as such: language. The organism's passage through and into language is castration, introducing the idea of loss and absence into the world.

THE SYMBOL OF THIS PASSAGE IS, AS ALWAYS, THE PHALLUS, THE WAY IN WHICH THE UNCONSCIOUS REPRESENTS THE IDEA OF LOSS.

Lacan's formulation has an important clinical implication.

IF JOUISSANCE IS REAL, OUTSIDE THE REGISTER OF IMAGE AND SYMBOLIC, HOW CAN PSYCHOANALYSIS ACT ON IT, GIVEN THAT ITS PRINCIPAL TOOL IS SPEECH?

The answer is contained in the thesis that what operates "shifts" in jouissance is language.

This automatically puts into question those therapies that think the organism can be fundamentally changed by non-symbolic practices.

This was one of Freud's preoccupations from his earliest psychoanalytic work in the 1890s.

I SAW THE PSYCHE AS A NETWORK OF REPRESENTATIONS IN WHICH A SUM OF EXCITATION WAS CONSTANTLY AT WORK.

The psyche had to find ways of dealing with this excess, principally by diverting it and providing new routes for it using the network of representations.

149

The Pass

In 1967, Lacan introduced a new practice into the field of psychoanalysis called the "pass". The end of analysis had been a topic of debate and controversy since the very start of organized psychoanalytic institutions, and Lacan's invention was designed **to offer literally a "pass" where others had only found "impasse"**.

This procedure was a bold innovation. It showed that analysis with one's personal analyst was not the closure of one's relation to psychoanalysis.

In telling the story of one's analysis to others, material could be ordered and set into place, new perspectives could emerge, even if this did not necessarily mean that one had "passed" as such.

The analytic experience was thus shown to extend beyond its traditional limits. The pass is still the subject of lively debate in the analytic community and constitutes one of the most interesting research areas of contemporary psychoanalysis, as people who have been analysed contribute material to the analytic community which otherwise would be shrouded in silence and obscurity. They try to explain what actually happened in their analysis, what the crucial moments of change were and where and why these occurred. Rather than relying on the erratic testimony of the books people occasionally write about their analysis, Lacan thus found a way of making the personal experience of psychoanalysis a part of the work of the analytical school itself.

The Events of May 1968

Unlike many other intellectuals, Lacan responded to the May Events of 1968 with neither the attitude of glorifying the student movement nor that of a timid distance. Respecting the strike call, he interrupted his seminar and held meetings with the students' leaders, including Daniel Cohn-Bendit. He signed a letter expressing solidarity with the students.

I won't mince my words. What you want is another master!

Indeed, maintaining his view that real revolutions start with ideas and formalizations, Lacan responded to the Events by devoting his seminar to analysing the structure of mastery itself. He produced formalizations of the four discourses which constitute the social bond.

LA LUTTE CONTINUE

Discourses of the master, the hysteric, the University and the analyst.

solidarité EFFECTIVE étudiants travailleurs

$$\frac{S_2}{S_1} \xrightarrow{U} \frac{a}{\$} \quad \frac{S_1}{\$} \xrightarrow{M} \frac{S_2}{a} \quad \frac{\$}{a} \xrightarrow{H} \frac{S_1}{S_2} \quad \frac{a}{S_2} \xrightarrow{A} \frac{\$}{S_1}$$

... EST DONNE

POUR UNE

LUTTE PROLONGEE

Lacan's popularity with the students and his putting in question established forms of power led to the withdrawal of his habitual seminar room at the École Normal Supérieure by its director in 1969. A protest immediately followed, and the director's office was occupied by several of those who regularly attended Lacan's seminars, including Antoinette Fouque, Julia Kristeva and Philippe Sollers. The seminar then continued at the Law Faculty on the Place du Panthéon

Lalangue

In the early 1970s, Lacan turned his attention more and more to the place of jouissance in human sexuality, the field he had discussed with such subtlety in the late 1950s with the theoretical tools of desire and the phallus. Whereas language and jouissance had remained distinct in most of his formulations until now, Lacan argued that **there is a side to language which is itself a form of jouissance**. If language was traditionally seen as made up of signifiers, each of which was linked to another signifier, he now proposed that there was a signifier without such links . . .

...a One, which makes up "lalangue", an amalgam of libido and signifiers.

Language is now shown to have not only effects of meaning and signification, but direct effects of jouissance. These ideas complicated the received notion that the libido and jouissance were different in nature from linguistic elements.

Logic of Sexuation

In the seminar "Encore", Lacan proposed what he called "formulas of sexuation" to set down the basic structures of male and female sexuality. In his book **Totem and Taboo**, Freud had argued that at the mythic origin of society lay a primal horde, in which a jealous and greedy father enjoyed all the women.

WE, HIS SONS, WERE DEPRIVED OF ALL INTERCOURSE WITH THEM.

AND SO WE REBELLED AND MURDERED OUR FATHER TO GAIN ACCESS TO THE WOMEN.

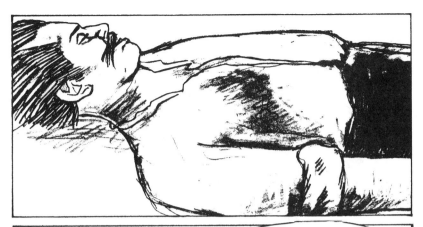

BUT THEN, IN REMORSE, WE FORBADE OURSELVES THE VERY WOMEN WE HAD MURDERED FOR.

THE FIRST LAW OF SOCIETY WAS THUS IMPOSED BY THE SONS ON THEMSELVES AS A RESULT OF THEIR LOVE AND REMORSE FOR THEIR MURDERED FATHER.

If this law is understood as a prohibition of jouissance, it is based, at its origin, on a jouissance which is obscene, perverse and unregulated — that of the primal father.

All Men . . .

Thus, Lacan argues that the law of prohibition always supposes at its horizon an exception, someone who escapes the law. If all men are subject to a law, one man escapes.

$$\forall x \, \overline{\Phi} x \qquad \exists x \, \overline{\overline{\Phi} x}$$

This structure is con-
stitutive of male sex-
uality.If all males are
subject to prohibition,
castration, there is at
least one who escapes.

If Freud's story in ***Totem and Taboo*** was a myth, **Lacan tries to extract a logical structure from it** and he gives notation for the sexuality.

Supplementary Jouissance

As Lacan pointed out there is no myth in the analytic literature like that contained in **Totem and Taboo** about female sexuality. According to Lacan, women participate in a logic very different from that of the man.

> Not all subjects are subject to castration, even if there does not exist a subject who is not subject to castration.

The jouissance of a speaking being may be phallic or it may be "supplementary", an enjoyment born out of the castration complex but not linked to the organ and its limits.

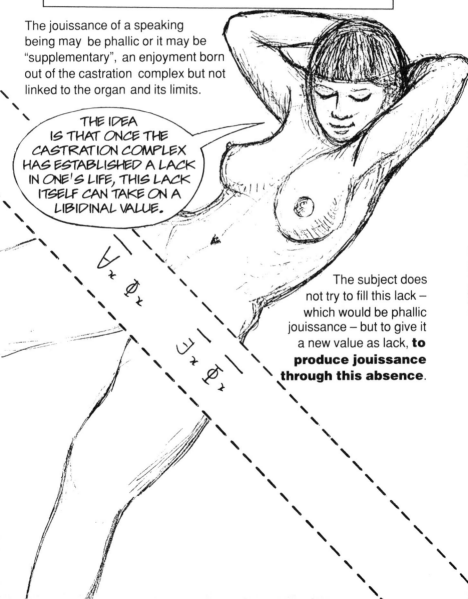

THE IDEA IS THAT ONCE THE CASTRATION COMPLEX HAS ESTABLISHED A LACK IN ONE'S LIFE, THIS LACK ITSELF CAN TAKE ON A LIBIDINAL VALUE.

The subject does not try to fill this lack – which would be phallic jouissance – but to give it a new value as lack, **to produce jouissance through this absence**.

Not-all

Men and women are both subject to the imposition of the symbolic order and the networks of signifiers.

Hence Lacan can say that women are "not-all" in the field of symbolic castration, even if the whole dynamic in question only exists owing to the initial presence of this symbolic dimension.

In Clinical Practice

Now, although these formulas seem amazingly abstract and distant from the world of clinical practice, they are not. If sexuality involves a sort of materialization of these structures in the associations brought by the patient, one can understand much of the data precisely as an attempt to introduce the formulas to which Lacan had given logical form.

I PERSISTED IN IDENTIFYING WITH A SERIES OF FAMOUS TYRANTS, AND THEN WHAT I CALLED "ALL THE MEN IN THE WORLD".

The clinical material shows that what is in question here is a privileging of people who, the child thinks, are outside the law and **occupy the place of exceptions**.

Although this child was caught in a world in which the Oedipal complex was hardly standard, we can see his attempt to set its structure in place, perhaps in a mad way, by incarnating the logic which it supposes: the exception and the rule.

FOR "ALL THE MEN IN THE WORLD" TO EXIST, THERE HAS TO BE AN EXCEPTION, THE TYRANT.

The logic of **Totem and Taboo** is thus given a new embodiment. Lacan's formulas are explanatory and useful in day-to-day clinical practice. Their elaboration shows Lacan's constant preoccupation with finding ways of formalising psychic processes.

Topology and Knots

Lacan's interest in mathematical techniques is a direct consequence of the way in which he conceived of the unconscious, even in his early work. If the unconscious is made up of relations between signifiers, **there must be an order or structure imposed on them**, which holds them together and organizes their relations. A signifier is a discrete element, different from other signifiers, and so may be taken as a component of a **set**. Now, a space is a set, a set of points, and hence **a network of signifiers would constitute a space**. Since mathematics offers many ways of investigating the properties of spaces, it was in this direction that Lacan moved. His early interest was in the properties of surfaces and then, in the 1970s, in knots, as we shall see.

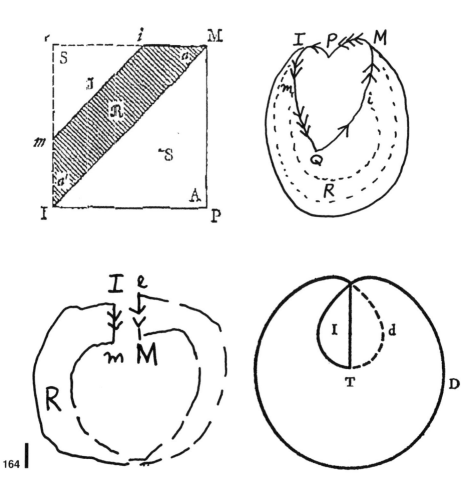

RSI

In the seminar "RSI", Lacan returned to study the relations of the three orders of **the real** (R), **the symbolic** (S) and **the imaginary** (I). In the 1950s, he had given a special priority to the symbolic, arguing that it was responsible for structuring the other two orders, but now he hypothesized a sort of **equivalence between the three orders**. What mattered was less one order's priority over others than the way they were linked. Lacan invoked the structure of certain knots to deepen this investigation, once again turning to mathematics for the formalizations he was seeking. Although this theorizing seemed and still seems to many to be abstruse and devoid of clinical relevance, Lacan was addressing real problems in practice, particularly with psychotic structures and what Anglo-Saxon clinicians might call the borderline. The idea in the 1950s had been that what keeps things in place, more or less, is the name of the father. This binds things together and guarantees, in some sense, the Oedipus complex. But now Lacan argues that it is less the name of the father as such that really matters than **any element or device that can bind together the three orders** of the real, the symbolic and the imaginary. There is thus a sort of functionalism at work in Lacan's argument.

It is less what the name of the father IS that counts than what it DOES. Which is to NAME.

Knots

This formulation is of great interest clinically since it allows one to understand the delusional constructions and inventions, in all senses of the word, of a psychosis. These may serve to bind together the real, the symbolic and the imaginary. Thus the well-known presence of machines, computers and products of science in certain psychotic systems may be explained in a new way. Objects may be used or invented to bind together elements of the body image (the imaginary), linguistic or computer circuitry (the symbolic), and extreme excitation or pain (the real). A successful psychotic system may thus be considered as a knot or, indeed, as a proper name, which ties together the three orders. We can see how Lacan is thus dealing with clinical considerations, especially given the fact that an understanding of this use of knots can give invaluable help in guiding work with psychotic patients.

Sinthome

Lacan gives a new name to the element which can serve to bind the three orders of real, symbolic and imaginary. He calls it the "sinthome", a word play in French which includes references to "symptom'", "saint" and "Saint Thomas". The idea of the knotting function of this element introduces new research problems since it addresses directly the old psychoanalytic and psychiatric question of **non-triggered psychosis**.

Seminar on Joyce

The theory of "sinthome" suggests that such subjects have found a way of knotting the real, the imaginary and the symbolic. Lacan investigated such knottings in the year-long seminar he gave on James Joyce in 1975–6. Joyce, he argued, would be an example of such a structure. His writing bound together the registers and **he became the sinthome himself** in the promotion of his own name.

THROUGH MY WRITING, I BECAME "JOYCE", THE NAME I WANTED ACADEMICS TO CONTINUE STUDYING FOR CENTURIES.

If Joyce's father had failed in some sense to name him, through his art **he literally named himself**.

The form of such knots is still being studied by the Lacanian psychoanalytic community. We can thus plot a passage in Lacan's work, from an emphasis on the father in the 1950s to the sinthome in the 1970s, a movement which perhaps responds precisely to the changing clinical picture we are presented with today and evokes the Lacanian reference in the 1938 **Encyclopédie** article to the decline of the paternal imago in modern civilization.

SINTHOME

Dissolution

In 1980, Lacan dissolved the EFP, the school of psychoanalysis he had founded some sixteen years earlier.

I felt that the transmission of psychoanalysis had become stagnant and that an inertia had descended on the analytic forum.

Lacan died on 9 September 1981.

Several new schools emerged from the dissolution of the EFP, and Lacan's work is continued today by psychoanalytic associations throughout the world. In Britain, the Centre for Freudian Analysis and Research provides seminars on Lacanian psychoanalysis with many speakers from Europe and beyond, and offers a training in Lacanian psychoanalysis (www.cfar.org.uk).

permis de développer de l'...
...é, s'accommode de sa transform...

$$f(S)\frac{1}{s}$$

la coprésence non seulement des éléments
horizontale, mais de ses attenances verti...
que nous avons ... les effets, répartis
fondamentales dans la métonymie et dans la
...vons les symboliser par :

$$f(S\dots S')\,S \cong S(-)s$$

...structure métonymique, indiquant que c'est la
...nifiant au signifiant qui permet l'élision par quo...
...stalle le manque de l'être dans la relation d'o...
...e la valeur de renvoi de la signification po...
...isant ce manque qu'il supporte. Le si...
...nifestant ici le maintien de la barre —, ...
...r marque l'irréductible où se co...
...u signifiant au signifié la résistance...
...maintenant :

$$f\left(\frac{S'}{S}\right)S \cong S(+)$$

...ructure métaphorique, indiquant que c'est dans la sub...
...on du signifiant au signifiant que se produit un effet de si...
...tion qui est de poésie ou de création, autrement dit d'a...
...nt de la signification en question. Le signe + placé entr...

Note on the Text

This book is an attempt to expound the work of Jacques Lacan. The material contained in balloons is not quotation unless it is set within quotation marks. Likewise, the clinical examples are only Lacan's when this is explicitly stated.

Further Reading

Books by Jacques Lacan

Lacan published his famous collection of articles, *Écrits* in 1966 (Norton, New York, 1977). There is an English version of part of the text *Écrits: A Selection*, (Norton, New York, 1977), but the translation is poor and this makes it a difficult place to start. Much more accessible are the translations of Lacan's seminars. These have been edited by Jacques-Alain Miller, and at present five have appeared in translation under the general title *The Seminars of Jacques Lacan*:

Seminar 1: "Freud's Papers on Technique", translated by John Forrester (Norton, New York, 1988).

Seminar 2: "The Ego in Freud's Theory and in the Technique of Psychoanalysis, translated by Sylvana Tomaselli (Norton, New York, 1988).

Seminar 3: "The Psychoses", translated by Russell Grigg (Norton, New York, 1993).

Seminar 7: "The Ethics of Psychoanalysis", translated by Dennis Porter (Norton, New York, 1992).

Seminar 11: "The Four Fundamental Concepts of Psychoanalysis", translated by Alan Sheridan (Norton, New York, 1977).

The *Écrits* becomes easier to read after studying the seminars. Many articles by Lacan have also appeared in translation. *Feminine Sexuality*, edited by Jacqueline Rose and Juliet Mitchell (Norton, New York, 1982), brings together translations of several papers on sexuality. Others which have appeared in translation are: "The Neurotic's Individual Myth" in *Psychoanalytic Quarterly* 48, 1979, pp. 405–425; "Some Reflections on the Ego" in the *International Journal of Psycho-Analysis*, 34, 1953, pp. 11–17; "Television" in *October* 40, 1987, a special issue which combines a translation of Lacan's television presentation with important documents on the debates linked to Lacan's relation with the International Psycho-Analytic Association and the dissolution of the École Freudienne de Paris. This issue is published in book form by Norton, New York, and contains other texts of interest, including correspondence with Winnicott. *October* also published a translation of the article "Kant with Sade" in issue 51, 1989, pp. 55–104.

Books on Lacan

The secondary literature on Lacan in English is becoming more and more extensive, yet until recently it has tended to be unreliable, neglecting the clinical aspect and relying frequently on secondary sources and partial surveys of the material. However, there are now *Reading Seminar XI: Lacan's Four Fundamental Concepts of Psychoanalysis*, edited by Richard Feldstein, Bruce Fink, Maire Jaanus (SUNY, Albany, 1995) and *Reading Seminars I and II: Lacan's Return to Freud*, (SUNY, Albany, 1995). Bruce Fink has also published the excellent *The Lacanian Subject* (Princeton University Press, 1995) and *A Clinical Introduction to Lacanian Psychoanalysis* (Harvard University Press, 1996), and Dylan Evans has published *An Introductory Dictionary of Lacanian Psychoanalysis* with Routledge in 1996. Bice Benvenuto and Roger Kennedy, *The Works of Jacques Lacan* (Free Association Books, London, 1986), is a good introduction. Slavoj Žižek's books *The Sublime Object of Ideology* (Verso, London, 1989) and *Looking Awry: An Introduction to Lacan through Popular Culture* (MIT Press, 1991) are also interesting and illuminating books in the field. Important articles and translations may be found in the English-language Lacanian journals, *Newsletter of the Freudian Field* (Missouri), *Analysis* (Melbourne, Australia) and *Journal of the Centre for Freudian Analysis and Research* (London).

Biography

The two main sources here are Elisabeth Roudinesco, *Jacques Lacan and Co.: A History of Psychoanalysis in France 1925–1985* (Free Association Books, London, 1990) and her biography of Lacan, *Jacques Lacan, Outline of a Life, History of a System of Thought* (Columbia University Press, 1994).

Acknowledgements

The approach to Lacan adopted in this book owes a great deal to the work of Jacques-Alain Miller. He has clarified and explained what is often difficult and apparently obscure, and he has stressed the historical consideration of the development of Lacan's thought. I wish to thank Anne Dunand, Richard Klein and Geneviève Morel for their comments and suggestions on my draft and Bernard Burgoyne whose comments on negative hallucination and on "Encore" I have used in the text. I am very grateful to Silvia Elena Tendlarz for the picture reproduced on page 13, which is taken from her thesis "Le cas Aimée: Étude historique et structurale", University of Paris VIII, 1989.

Darian Leader

Judy Groves would like to thank Naomi Lobbenberg, Joanna and Max Peters, Maya Magoga-Aranovich, David King, Howard Selina, Howard Peters, Peter Groves and Claudine Meissner for their invaluable help in the production of this book.

Darian Leader is a psychoanalyst practising in London. He is the author of *Why Do Women Write More Letters Than They Post?* (1996), *Promises Lovers Make When It Gets Late* (1998), *Freud's Footnotes* (2000) and *Stealing the Mona Lisa: What Art Stops Us From Seeing* (2002), all published by Faber & Faber.

Judy Groves is a painter, graphic designer and illustrator. She has also illustrated *Philosophy, Christianity, Wittgenstein, Plato, Lévi-Strauss* and *Chomsky* in this series.

Typeset by Wayzgoose
Balloon lettering by Woodrow Phoenix

Index